Faith For The Next Step

52 Messages To Inspire And Encourage

Loretta McNary

Five Seven Media Publishing
Memphis, TN 38115

Scripture quotations from The Message/ Amplified/ King James Version/21st Century King James Version/American Standard Bible/New American Standard Bible/New International Version/New Living Translation

ISBN: 978-0-9841096-0-9
ISBN: 0-9841096-0-9

Library of Congress Catalog Publication Data 2011914220
Printed in the United States of America

Cover Design by Ken Norfork

Faith For The Next Step

52 Messages To Inspire And Encourage

Dedication

Unto Him who knew me before the beginning of time, my heavenly Father, my eternal gratitude. You are a mighty and loving God. May this book be to others what it has definitely been for me, the encouragement I need on a tough day, and an amazing spiritual catalyst that helps lead us straight to You.

This labor of love is dedicated to my father, Dave Shorter, Jr. (R.I.P. February 17, 1999), my son, Brandon Maurice McNary (R.I.P. July 15, 1999). I will always cherish their lives. And I will always remember their unconditional love and tireless support of me and my business endeavors. Thank you so much for the wisdom you so freely shared with me whenever I needed it the most.

To my mother, Dorothy Shorter-Peggs, you are my first and best role model. To my sons, Marshall, Nicholas, Spencer, and Jacob, thank you for unselfishly allowing me to pursue my dreams.

And, finally but not least, to parents who have had to bear the extreme grip of grief and pain caused by experiencing the passing of a child. May you always trust God to carry you until you have the strength and faith you need for your next step.

Table of Contents

Acknowledgements

To my Heavenly Father whose love, wisdom, favor, mercy and grace are everlasting, and all I need to live moment-by-moment and day-by-day. I am forever grateful to you, Lord, for choosing me for such a time as this. Without you, Father, none of what I do would be possible.

To Brandon, who because of his undying love, support, and faith, I am now becoming the woman I was created to become. To Marshall, who has been a constant strength and shoulder to lean on during the tough times. To Nicholas, who continues to teach me to take time to enjoy life more and to look deeper inside my soul for the answers. To Spencer, whose determination to be true to his own unique identity encourages me to be true to mine. To Jacob, whose passion to have the desires of his heart inspires me to dream bigger dreams too.

And to my mother, her silent strength liberates me to seek and find the inner strength I need on those days that seem to challenge me the most. And to my earthly Father, who was taken from me way too soon, your strong work ethics and your essence of treating everyone with kindness and respect, that you instilled in me shape and mold me daily.

And a special thanks to my brother, Larry McNary, and my sister, Wanda McNary Parker-Brown; and my sister-in-law, Laura McNary thanks for loving me through all of my trials and triumphs of life.

To all of my nieces, nephews, grand nieces, and grand-nephews I love you all so much and am praying for you all to seek and walk in your individual purpose. And to the rest of my entire family, both on my father's side and on my mother's side, your love, and support is deeply appreciated and reciprocated.

A hearty and special thank you to all of my closest friends for all of your prayers, support, and friendship; I am both very grateful and thankful. A very special thanks to Janice Gatewood, Janice Ousley, Juanita Dillard, Kathy Blake, Tony Johnson, Tawonda & Darren Echols, Shelia E. Lipsey, Glenn A. Hill, James Robinson, Jr., Loretta Tyree, Dr. Maurice Tyree, Veda Howse, Danny & Amelia Cole, Pastor Craig Strickland, Dr. Eli Morris, Mary Ann Ruff, Mr. and Mrs. Jason Farmer, Andy Kuhl, Mr. Luke Yancy, III, Gwen Jordan & Family, Terry Digel, Edith Kelly-Green, Ken and Jaye Norfork, Ruby Bright, Shelby County Sheriff's Office, Ruby Davis, Pastor and Mrs. Chuck Moscato, Faye & Howard Bynum, Jennifer Kiesewetter, To my church family at Hope Presbyterian Church, whose faith often helped to carry me when my own faith was not enough for my next step.

Last, a big thanks to Shelia E. Lipsey for editing my first book, *Faith for the Next Step*. Thank you for your professional generosity and for believing in this book from the very start and for walking with me every step of the way. I appreciate you.

Foreword by Dr. Eli Morris

If there is a word that describes the condition of so many of us these days, the word is "discouragement." And as much as we may try to make ourselves happy and content, so often those efforts fall short.

They fall short because most of our efforts at happiness only address the surface of our discouragement. We put "band-aids" on our broken spirit rather than address the core of our problem. Therefore, we spend money we do not have. We make promises we cannot keep. We commit to people we do not love.

Several years ago, I met one of the most encouraging people I have ever encountered. Her name is Loretta McNary, and her joy and optimism come from a deep and relevant spiritual walk that she has nurtured through a life that has been far from perfect. Perhaps that is part of the secret of her encouraging spirit.

Loretta has seen such significant pain, that she had to decide whether her Faith was real enough to lift her heart out of the darkness and into the light. Fortunately, for all of us, Loretta found that God can in fact give us a heart of hope.

In this book, Loretta McNary takes us through 52 weeks of encouragement and empowerment. We have the opportunity to spend a year walking away from our discouragement and walking toward God's encouraging presence.

I pray that you will engage in this journey of renewal as Loretta shares both from her life and from God's Word.

Under His mercy,
Dr. Eli Morris
Pastor of Urban Ministry
Hope Church
Memphis, TN

Introduction

Faith For The Next Step
52 Messages To Inspire And Encourage

Bad days, tough days whatever you call a day that brings sadness, depression, disappointment, and despair, first starts with a bad moment. The good news is we are in control of how long a bad moment lasts. We can control whether a bad moment becomes a bad hour, a bad day, a bad month or a bad year.

We have the power to change a bad moment into a better moment with our thoughts, reactions, and decisions. Yes, bad things do happen to good people. I am a living witness and I am sure many of you are too. I have experienced the death of my father and my first-born son. I have had a car repossessed; a fire at a neighbor's house destroyed my apartment, along with everything we owned; and I have been unemployed. Matter of fact, some of these things happened within a few months or within one year of each other.

I am not promising that reading this book will be everything you need to have faith for the next step. However, I know that if we practice and actively use the information in this book, we can learn to minimize negative reactions and responses, and learn what not to do so that we no longer empower the bad moments to become bad days. I am not saying that the information written in this book is a magic wand or anything remotely powerful in of itself, or that your life will be easier if you read this book. Nor am I telling you to just "get over it" and pretend that you are happy. I am simply saying that, you have the power to control the amount of time that you feel sorry or bad about some non-life threatening event that brings disappointments into your day. As the song goes, sometimes, *you have to encourage yourself.*

Of course there may be times and some situations or incidents that warrant *a just get over it.* However, let me tell you, grieving over the death of a loved one is definitely not one of those instances. I can assure you that everyone grieves and handles grief differently. If someone tells you how to grieve and when and how long to grieve, tell them to back off. The sad, hurt feelings and the heartache caused by the death of a loved one, can sometimes last a lifetime. Of course, there are many exceptions to this statement, if you or someone you know is going through or experiencing an extreme and prolonged depression; this is a different story, because that person may need to seek professional help. If so, I urge you to seek help immediately.

Anyway, I decided to write this book for several other reasons, which includes wanting to help people feel better about their own lives regardless of their current circumstance. My desire is to be a catalyst in pointing people to the path that is filled with joy. The right path for me leads me to Jesus. I am a firm believer that I am who I am and have been able to overcome some serious trials and tribulations only through His grace and mercy. What helps in any situation is having *Faith for the Next Step.*

FAITH

Now faith is the substance of things hoped for and the evidence of things not seen. Hebrews 11:1 (King James Version)

My first realization of the kind of faith described in Hebrews 11:1, began with my first ever epiphany. In August 2006, the Lord gave me a vision. In this vision, I actually saw myself on stage hosting and interviewing guests seated on a couch in front of an audience. Also in the vision, I was told that my show would be very similar to the #1 rated, nationally syndicated TV talk show at the time. The only stipulation was that my talk show would be done from a Christian perspective. However, it was not to be preachy or fanatical. It simply means that in addition to the national format and topics, pastors, and choirs are also invited to be guests on the show. On December 6, 2006, I hosted the very first Loretta McNary TV Talk Show in front of an audience of about 100 people. In December 2011, I will be celebrating my fifth year of hosting the Loretta McNary Show.

Through hosting the show, I have learned firsthand the real definition of faith. Faith has two friends that must exist simultaneously. They are: *believe* and *work*. You really have to believe, without a shadow of doubt, that what you need and want will manifest in your life.

Regardless of how things look, feel and appear at the moment, regardless of your lack of experience, money, or know how, if you believe enough to begin the work to make it happen, your faith will activate the manifestation of your dreams. It has been said many times that I have "crazy" faith. I am not really sure what people mean when they say that because to me, I simply have an active faith. Instead of an *if only* faith which I notice many people have today. They say *if only* I had more money, *if only* the children were old enough, *if only* my husband or wife, *if only* I had a husband/wife, *if only* I could lose the weight. Waiting for things to get better is not faith. What I refer to as an active faith or a right now faith, is the kind of faith that will push you past all of the excuses of *if only*.

Having right now faith for me means embracing and practicing daily the embodiment of trust and obedience. Without faith, life can sometimes become overwhelmingly difficult. During difficult times or days, you may have asked yourself "Is my life worth living"? I have asked this question in my life more than a few times. On those days, I have found when I do the four following simple things, it makes a world of difference in my attitude:

1. Take some time to be silent. I encourage you to find a safe place to be still and quiet.

2. Do not make any major decisions when you experience this feeling of worthlessness and despair.

3. Do what needs to be done that day without procrastinating, especially when you really would rather not do anything.

4. Find your voice of praise. Think of things that are good, kind, loving, and positive in your life. Sometimes just simply saying these two words, *thank you* is enough to move you into a state of feeling better about your circumstances. These two simple words "thank you" have a way of cleansing and comforting your mind.

You might ask, Loretta, have there been times when you felt you did not have enough faith for a situation? The answer is of course, yes. There have been many times. It usually happens when I am feeling overwhelmed because things are not happening as fast as I want them to or exactly like I planned. One thing I know for sure is it is extremely important to remember to be grateful for the things you already have, especially in the midst of feeling as if your faith is gone or that you just do not have enough. There have been countless days when I felt like nothing was going right, or a feeling of lack was taking over my thoughts and really challenged my faith. Staying in the moment allowed me to be less stressed, which coincidentally helped me to regain my faith. Living in the moment also encouraged me to validate my true feelings. Another lesson I learned that helps increase and sustain my faith is remembering the many times in the past when I had mountain moving faith, and God allowed me to overcome the challenges I may have been facing that day. Being obedient and trusting God's Word and His promises produced the strong *right now* faith I now enjoy. Now I have the faith, the belief that things will get better soon, even in the face of trouble, sadness, and in a season of *not enough*.

Here is another example of how trusting and being obedient to God's Word and power helped increase my faith so that I could overcome an extremely tough time in my past. My father, who died February 17, 1999 (just 5 months before my oldest son, Brandon, died) often said, 'What doesn't kill you will make you stronger'. I have found this to be true on numerous occasions. I will always remember that *right now* faith sometimes can only be truly developed through times of adversity.

Our faith, much like the muscles in our physical bodies, tends to become much stronger the more we use it. Faith put in action in good times and in difficult times can increase your faith. *Right now* faith is more powerful and becomes more easily available when troubled times arise. Remember, that God is always faithful. In the Old Testament book of Psalms 100:5 (New International Version) it states, *For the LORD is good and his love endures forever; his faithfulness continues through all generations.*

This week's mantra: My faith will produce a harvest equal to my works and beliefs!

Week 2

Hope

So God has given both his promise and his oath. These two things are unchangeable because it is impossible for God to lie. Therefore, we who have fled to him for refuge can have great confidence as we hold to the hope that lies before us. Hebrews 6:18 (New Living Translation)

Here is my bold statement on hope; Hope anchors the soul. Hope is the total belief and surrender that God's Word is true. Which brings me to my next bold statement: Never, ever give up hoping that things will work out or that things will get better in your life somehow. One thing I know for sure about hope is that it is much like love—like love, hope begets more of itself. You have probably heard it many times to *never give up hope*. For some, this statement has a lot of relevance. It is likened to food and water, which brings nourishment to the body. The soul needs hope to survive. In the midst of any storm, trouble, or tribulation; hope is the lighthouse, the anchor and the rope to grab hold to. Hope can guide you through the turbulent waters and keep the massive waves from taking you under. Hope can be the bridge over troubled waters. Hope can be the spiritual shelter from a storm that comes up fast, unexpectedly and suddenly in your life.

My hope is in God, and this hope is available to everyone who believes. Hope is priceless and yet available in abundance. It only costs you what it gives so freely, more hope. Hope is never illusive or hidden. Yet, when we are feeling down, depressed, lonely and in despair, hope seems like the last thing we want to hear about or hang on to. Yet, it is the very thing that can change a life, redirect a life, save a life, and support a life. Hope is impartial. It does not care who grabs a hold of it. It freely gives to those who seek and hold on to it. It is an equalizer. It is sometimes the difference between having peace and not having peace in our life.

On those rare occasions when you just feel like you cannot make it one more day or hour, or that you just want peace in a situation, I dare you to say, "My hope is in God, and I know everything will work out for my good." I know for sure that hope activated gives you the strength you need to make it through until the situation is made better. I pray that you will embrace hope and offer it to others as often as it is needed.

This week's mantra: The things I hope for are the things I expect daily!

JOY

For his anger lasts only a moment, but his favor lasts a lifetime! Weeping may last through the night, but joy comes with the morning. Psalms 30:5 (New Living Translation)

Joy is definitely a surreal state of being that is worth seeking day and night. Although joy sometimes seems alien to us, joy resides within us regardless of what is going on around us. Our joy is always waiting on us to acknowledge its presence. It was not until I learned to acknowledge the joy that lives within me that my life started to look a whole lot better. I started to appreciate all that I have and everything I was going through. However, choosing joy is an everyday choice. Just like choosing to have faith and hope, we have to choose joy daily and oftentimes moment-by-moment.

Prior to learning the difference between happiness and joy, I sometimes confused happiness with joy. When good things happened in my life or someone did something nice for me like buying me a present, then I thought those things caused me joy. However, I later learned that happiness is an emotional state of being that is a chosen response based on external circumstances, i.e. when something happens that is good, that makes you smile, or laugh, or someone gives you a compliment. Happiness is based simply on emotions, and emotions only. Those emotions are triggered by outside sources.

As for joy, joy comes from within. Joy originates from having an active relationship with our heavenly Father. Real joy is not based on life's situations, temporary circumstances, or whether you feel things are going good or bad. Joy is more of a spiritual nature. It is not influenced by present or future weather forecasts or predictions, or whether your finances are secure or unpredictable, or if you have lost your job or you are gainfully employed. Once you experience real joy, you will find that joy cannot be changed or lost at a moment's notice. It is embedded in your spirit, your soul, and your being. Only God can bestow joy in your life. And He dispenses it freely when you ask.

In order to live a well-balanced, less stress-filled life, connect with your joy that resides within you every day in every situation. When you are feeling despondent, in despair or empty, ask God to, *"Restore to me the joy of your salvation and grant me a willing spirit, to sustain me (Psalm 51:12 NIV).*

We cannot get by today on yesterday's joy. We need joy daily, like breathing. Once we embrace joy, we will begin to be less reactive and more proactive in making our dreams come true. This has proven true in my life and in the lives of those I shared my experiences with in the past. Believe me; joy does come in the morning, at noonday and in the midnight hour. Joy is perfected peace. Reach out and welcome the joy that only a loving, and gracious God can give.

This week's mantra: The joy I have was not given by man nor can man take it away!

PEACE

So God has given both his promise and his oath. These two things are unchangeable because it is impossible for God to lie. Therefore, we who have fled to him for refuge can have great confidence as we hold to the hope that lies before us. Hebrews 6:18 (New Living Translation)

Peace, like faith, hope and joy is what I empower to reign in my life. When both my dad and son died in 1999, I learned many valuable lessons. The first one is having Jesus is truly worth more than gold even when you have lots of friends and family around you.

Secondly, the mind is a very interesting and powerful thing. It can cause you to see and feel things differently. Your mind actually influences what you really see with your eyes, as does your heart. However, because of the faultiness of the heart, having peace in your mind is an equally important by-product for your *Faith for the Next Step*.

As you know, sometimes things do not work out as planned. The difference between getting over an undesired outcome and not getting over an undesired outcome is having peace in your heart and mind. This is especially true when you have to make a decision that some people around you may not understand or support based on the desired outcome. Having peace that you did the best you could, depending on the facts you had at the time, makes all the difference in the world. Sometimes, well let me say, many times. I have trouble falling asleep and staying asleep. After enduring many years of sleepless nights, I began to pray about this and discovered that because I did not have peace about a particular situation that was going on in my life, I became sleep deprived. Now I totally understand the value of not going to bed angry, filled with worry or frustration. It is very difficult to enjoy a good night of sleep if you do not have peace in your mind and in your heart.

Here is a story by Arun Gandhi. It is titled "What is Peace?" I would like to share it with you.

A favorite story that grandfather liked to tell us was the story of an ancient Indian king who was obsessed with the desire to find the meaning of peace. What is peace, and how can we get it? And when we find it, what should we do with it were some of the issues that bothered him. Intellectuals in his kingdom were invited to answer the king's questions for a handsome reward. Many tried but none could explain how to find peace and what to do with it. At last, someone said the king ought to consult the sage who lived just outside the borders of his kingdom:

"He is an old man and very wise," the king was told. "If anyone can answer your questions, he can."

The king went to the sage and posed the eternal question. Without a word, the sage went into the kitchen and brought a grain of wheat to the king. "In this you will find the answer to your question," the sage said as he placed the grain of wheat in the king's outstretched palm.

Puzzled, but unwilling to admit his ignorance, the king clutched the grain of wheat and returned to his palace. He locked the precious grain in a tiny gold box and placed the box in his safe. Each morning, upon waking, the king would open the box and look at the grain to seek an answer but could find nothing.

Weeks later, another sage passing through, stopped to meet the king who eagerly invited him to resolve his dilemma. The king explained how he had asked the eternal question and the sage had given him a grain of wheat instead. "I have been looking for an answer every morning, but I find nothing."

The sage said, "It is quite simple, your highness. Just as this grain represents nourishment for the body, peace represents nourishment for the soul. Now, if you keep this grain locked up in a gold box it will eventually perish without providing nourishment or multiplying. However, if it is allowed to interact with the elements of light, water, air, and soil it will flourish, multiply and soon you would have a whole field of wheat, which will nourish not only you, but so many others. This is the meaning of peace. It must nourish your soul and the souls of others; it must multiply by interacting with the elements."

Peace is another God given gift. Without peace, your troubles appear multiplied significantly. Without peace, even the smallest of problems that arise in our lives, appear as giants! Pray and ask God for the kind of peace only He is able to give. Peace that goes beyond our human understanding is the type of peace I am talking about. Understand that if you do not *know peace* you will have *no peace*. Trust me, I have tried unsuccessfully more times than I care to share with you right now, and it was useless. Do not let this happen to you. Learn from my mistakes, it will save you from many sleepless nights.

This week's mantra: I receive the peace of God in my life today and forevermore.

LOVE

Love is patient and kind. Love is not jealous or boastful or proud or rude. It does not demand its own way. It is not irritable, and it keeps no record of being wronged. It does not rejoice about injustice but rejoices whenever the truth wins out. Love never gives up, never loses faith, is always hopeful, and endures through every circumstance. Three things will last forever—faith, hope, and love—and the greatest of these is love. I Corinthians 13:4-7, 13 (New Living Translation)

What is love really? Does anyone really know what love looks like or feels like? I began to learn the true meaning of love after the birth of my first-born son, Brandon. Brandon came into my world on May 12, 1983. Until I was blessed with my sons, I realized that I only loved with conditional love. I loved only if my needs and wants were being met, such as when, and if, I required something from another person. If they made me angry or upset or let me down, unconsciously, I decided to withhold my love for them until my demands were met. Sometimes it took a few minutes, hours or sometimes days, but until I was happy, I refused to shower my love upon that individual. I know this may sound a lot like *love for sale*, but I must speak the truth because it was how I use to measure my emotional love for others. I often found myself saying, if you loved, you would do this, or if you loved me you would not have done that or you would not have said that, and the list goes on. It was all about me and my self-gratification. The amount of love I dispensed was based on what or how a person acted or reacted toward what I wanted and expected of them.

Perhaps, you have heard hundreds of sermons, and may have read the chapter in the Bible on love quite a few times. Some call it the *love* chapter: I Corinthians 13. A few years ago, I decided to reread I Corinthians 13 for the umpteenth time, and I finally got it. Something clicked in my mind and my spirit. I was finally able to understand the real and true meaning of love. WOW! However, can I really love like that? I started to think that if I love like that what if the other person does not love me back in the same way. Well, apparently, I still did not get it. A few years and many sermons later, with the help of the Holy Spirit, I realized that, sure I can, if I can love my beloved sons, unconditionally, then surely I can learn to love others unconditionally.

Sidebar: I have to share an ugly truth with you. In the past, I am sure that sometimes some of my actions caused my sons to feel like I withheld my true, unconditional love from them no matter how temporary. Bad Mommy, I know, and I am ashamed. The truth is I never stopped loving them, not ever, but if they made me angry or disappointed, I treated them differently, I got quiet, I pouted, and sometimes I was blunt in my response and remarks. However, I am sure that this translated to them and felt like I did stop loving them, for the moment. And, yes, I have repented and asked for forgiveness many times. As soon I received the revelation about this, I immediately took the time to learn to be a better parent and not allow my emotions rule me. They constantly reassure me that they know I love them unconditionally and they love me unconditionally too!

The encouraging news is we have a prime example, great instructions and easy to follow directions on how to get this love thing right. The greatest example is found in the way our heavenly Father loves us unconditionally with patience, kindness, no score keeping, no bragging, but with forgiveness and forever. Amazing, isn't it! Even with my newfound knowledge, I sometimes revert to my old way of loving others, not my sons though. Okay, before you judge me, and tsk tsk, remember; God is not through with me yet. Please know I am doing much better now. This proves that we are certainly capable of loving others unconditionally. I will be the first to admit that it does take a lot of prayer, commitment, and dedication, but we can get love right if we try, and only by remembering how much God loves us unconditionally.

This week's mantra: Perfected love abides in me and I am learning to share it unconditionally.

Week 6

SELF-LOVE

For the whole law can be summed up in this one command: "Love your neighbor as yourself. Galatians 5:14 *(New Living Translation)*

In the previous week we talked about the importance and commission of loving others unconditionally. "Do you really love yourself?" For me this is a really deep and profound question; one that only we can answer individually. Please be honest with yourself. I want to share a little unknown truth. Until my 40th birthday, I honestly did not truly love myself completely. Thankfully, no one knew this little dark secret of mine but me. Or at least this is what I like to think.

If you asked ten people who have known me for many years, I would venture to say that all ten would unanimously say yes, Loretta does love herself, matter of fact she loves herself a whole lot. Also around my 40th birthday, I realized that I am quite the actress whenever I need and want to be. However, one day it hit me like a ton of bricks that I was only performing. I was wearing the proverbial mask. And I was very good at applying my mask daily. I had become a master at masking my true feelings. I could talk the talk and even walk the walk, but after a lot of soul searching and painfully looking back at my life, it was so agonizingly obvious to me, that I really did not love myself. I did not have self-hate, but I did not have self-love either. I realized that I loved everybody else, even those who did not really love me. Yet, I did not love Loretta McNary. Oh my goodness, what a hard revelation to admit, but until I could admit that I did not love myself, I could not begin to truly love myself.

So here comes birthday number 40, and a new profound realization strikes me at the core of my very being—that I did not truly love me, nor did I really know me. Sounds absurd doesn't it? I started immediately to pray. I prayed for wisdom. I prayed for revelation about how this happened in my life. I also prayed to be shown what I needed to do about it. My answer was simply: forgive. Forgive? Forgive is exactly what I asked of God, my Father. The answer began to clearly unfold. I was told to start by forgiving myself of all the hurtful things I said about myself; forgive myself for not taking better care of me. I had to forgive myself for all of the times I allowed some man to enter my life without honoring me enough, or love me enough, to see that I was hurting deep inside from past relationships, and bad decisions. I had to forgive myself for not having the courage to allow myself to walk away from an unhealthy relationship and begin my healing process. I had to forgive myself for not allowing the healing process to begin. I had to forgive myself of all the times I questioned my value and self-worth. I could go on and on. But the truth remains that loving me did not come easy. Forgiving me did not come easy. Matter of fact, I would forgive myself and then turn right around and do the very same thing over and over that caused the hurt in the first place.

Thank God that I am finally in a special and much healthier place after that long process of soul searching and healing. Please excuse my broken English but now I can truly say; I *do love me some Loretta McNary*. It is not a vanity type of love that I have; it's so much deeper than that. It is not a shallow, uppity love that I have for myself for it is much broader than that. It's not based on the good that I do or the wrong that I wish I did not do, it goes much higher than that. It's a love that has been shown to me by God. Not only do I love me, I know why I love me now. God says. He loves me. God knows everything about me; all my secrets, all of my fears, all of the things I've done that weren't right, all the times I knowingly committed wrong against myself and others, all about my shortcomings and my midnight tears. God knows everything about me and yet He loves me. And since I trust His judgment, I figure I am worth loving. I hope and pray that you too will trust His judgment, and love yourself unconditionally. Began to see yourself in the manner in which God sees you. Began to look in the mirror and see beyond the outward layer and see deep within your heart, your soul. Refuse to allow defeat, and problems, and troubles, and mistakes and physical attributes or the lack thereof, influence you to dislike who God made you to be. Think about it. God created you. You are fearfully and wonderfully made. You are special. You are God's creation. We are worthy of being loved and of loving yourself.

The gift of learning to love me more leads to learning to love others unconditionally too. And this is the best place to be, embracing and loving who you are daily.

This week's mantra: God's love for me says it all, and I believe all He says about me!

FAMILY

"And now, O Lord God, I am your servant; do as you have promised concerning me and my family. Confirm it as a promise that will last forever." 2 Samuel 7:25 (New Living Translation)

For the sake of our journey together, your family is more inclusive than just your biological family. Family also consists of people you choose to include in your family structure. Family can include friends, those who choose to love you just for who you are nothing more nothing less.

A "family" dynamic will look different inside each home. Sometimes a family has a biological father, mother, and biological siblings living in the same household. Other times it is only the mother and children or a father and children. Yet, other times it is a grandparent raising grandchildren, or maybe an aunt/uncle raising their nieces and nephews, or foster parents raising children. Perhaps there are stepparents within a family helping to raise children. Whatever the case, please rest assured that your family is still a "family" in every sense of the word, regardless of the current make-up. Regardless of your family structure, you are whole, loved, and valued.

I have read hundreds of successful stories about individuals who are quite accomplished and wealthy, and were raised without their biological mothers or fathers in the household. I have heard of thousands of individuals who were raised in single-family households who lived in poverty that are now extremely successful and affluent.

My philosophy on this is if they can do this, so can millions of others who now live in, or once lived in similar circumstances. I say this to you, my sons, and friends, as often as I can, it is not where you start in life, but where you finish that counts the most.

So, today let us start being more grateful for the family we have and proud that they choose to love and care for us every day.

This week's mantra: My family may not be perfect, yet God loves us all

PURPOSE

So I run with purpose in every step. I am not just shadow-boxing. I Corinthians 9:26 (New Living Translation)

My definition of purpose is doing the thing that we were created to do in this world that no other person can do. Each one of us was created for a purpose. We are not just on the earth to enjoy the wonderful creations and the beauty of the earth. We are not accidents or the result of a careless mistake. We were put on earth to fulfill a mission. This divine mission ensures we have everything we will need to fulfill our purpose on this earth. As the great poet, Marianne Williams says, "Greatness is in all of us, not just in some of us."

How do you find what your individual purpose is? I am so elated that you asked. This question is one of the million dollar questions, but it can and must be answered. And regardless of how far-fetched this may sound to you at this time, you can find the answer through prayer, perhaps some fasting and a lot of determination.

First, I would suggest praying that question to God. Secondly, I would read what God says about divine purpose and calling in the Bible. Thirdly, I recommend you read as many reputable, Bible-based books that you can find on the subject of *purpose*, to help you get started on seeking, identifying and pursuing your purpose.

I can tell you this, purpose is usually found in using your God–given talents to help other people. It will also be associated with what you do that is very easy and natural for you to do, and other people will often compliment you on how well you did the "thing". Then you should continue to use the "thing" to be a blessing to others.

After I discovered and cataloged what my gifts and natural talents were, I intentionally began to use them to be a blessing to other people more frequently. So from then on, I immediately put into practice my speaking and exalting gifts - inspiring, educating, and empowering women and teens through the media using print, radio, and TV.

To get you started on your path to acknowledging and using your divine purpose begin by asking yourself today:

1. What do I do really well and effortless, yet the same thing would challenge most people?

2. What do other people say I am really good at?

3. What do I enjoy doing, even when hours have past and I am still enjoying the task?

The answers to these questions and continued prayer will motivate you to seek and pursue your purpose. Once you determine your true purpose, begin to work in your purpose. The world is depending and waiting on you.

Our individual purposes are so interconnected to one another's that if you are not living and working in your purpose, it impedes someone else from living and working in theirs.

We are so important to God and this world; that we all were *created on purpose, with a purpose, for a purpose.*

This week's mantra: When I pursue my purpose with intense passion, I discover my unlimited potential.

Words

Death and life are in the power of the tongue...Proverbs 18:21a (New American Standard Bible). Calling those things that are not as though they were...Romans 4:17c-d (New American Standard Bible)

I am sure you have heard the childhood nursery rhyme, "Sticks and stones may break my bones, but words will never hurt me." Well, I am not sure what inspired the writer to coin the phrase of this particular rhyme. Perhaps it was based on their own personal experiences with bullying. Yet, as a little girl, I was taught this rhyme as a retort to get back at the child who said mean and hurtful words to me or about me. Back then it seemed to have worked, at least from a ten-year-old girl's point of view. My feelings were hurt because someone called me a "four-eyed nerd" the first day I started wearing my glasses. I must have believed that if repeated this rhyme to them, it would prove that they were messing with the wrong little girl, a little girl who did not care what they said. Especially since my mother and father always reinforced to me that they were just mad because I was intelligent and beautiful. (What would we do without our loving, protective, and caring parents?)

However, one thing I can say for certain is that negative words do have the potential to hurt sometimes temporarily, sometimes permanently. I will even venture to say that sometimes words can and have hurt as much if not more, than a stick or a stone. Words also have awesome restoring and healing power. They can work for your good and they can also work against you. Their power is fueled by the tongue. Some of you, like me, have experienced the power of words that wound, hurt, and destroy. Words, once released, can never be taken back. You can apologize, beg for forgiveness, and have regrets about what you said to or about someone. Even though the person may forgive you, the memory of the words you spoke may linger for a while.

Words have soothing powers too. Words can produce faith or fear, defeat or victory. They have the power to change your life, and your future. They can also help you to align yourself with God and His will for your life. It's all in the words you speak.

I can remember many other times when the words of others hurt my feelings and caused me to feel bad about myself. I am equally aware that I have said words that caused someone else to doubt their worth as well. (Even now, I ask for forgiveness of those that I may have hurt with my words in the past.) Now I fully believe what the good Lord says about me in His word. He says, I am the head and not the tail, I am above not beneath, and I am more than a conqueror. These are words I can happily live with hearing on a daily basis.

Not only can words hurt our feelings they can also create our past, present and future circumstances, good or bad. The words we allow to come out of our mouths have so much power. They actually connect the natural world to the spiritual world. I could write this entire book on this principle alone. Be very careful of the words you choose to think and speak out loud about yourself, your loved ones, and others. We really do have the power to speak life or death. So from this point on, humor me. In case the things we speak really do come true, then please do not waste your time and energy speaking things out loud that you really do not want to happen.

Dr. Kenneth E. Hagin said, "Faith begins where the will of God is known." You must know the Word of God in order to believe what the Word says. The Word of God contains the power within itself to cause what it says to come to pass. If you believe God's Word, and you use it the way God intended for you to use it, then the Word will begin to work in your life. You must act on the Word. Faith is an act. The best way to begin to act on the Word is to speak the Word out loud!"

This week's mantra: I am building a great future with each word I speak!

Loretta McNary

Week 10

WAITING

But they that wait upon the LORD shall renew their strength; they shall mount up with wings as eagles; they shall run, and not be weary; and they shall walk, and not faint. Isaiah 40:31(King James Version)

Let me start out by saying, waiting does not mean inaction. Okay, we have that out of the way. For the purpose of this principle, I would like to point out that although the words patience and waiting are sometimes used interchangeably. However, to me they are two very separate concepts and principles.

I'm sure you have heard the phrase, "Patience is a virtue." Well, so is waiting. Yet, one is active and one can be passive. Let me explain.

For most of us, we recognize and admit we have a problem with patience. Yet, waiting is viewed so differently to many of us. Very few people admit I have a problem waiting. We think waiting is different from having patience. Having patience to me means you are okay in the process of where a situation or thing stands current-

29

ly. You are simply not experiencing the desired outcome or thing yet and are comfortable with this phase until the desired outcome is reached. So we say we are being patient. Or are we? How many times have we said "I am going to be patient" yet we continue to try to manipulate the circumstances and people involved to kind of hurry things along? That is neither patience nor waiting. I am so guilty of saying I am patient when in actuality I am not.

On the other hand, being patient and waiting can mean the anticipation of or the expected arrival of a thing hoped for. Being patience can mean waiting on something to happen. But waiting on a thing does not necessarily mean I am patient. Waiting means, stop-doing things to cause the thing you want and desire to happen by your own power. It means giving up trying to control things to force your desired outcome. Whereas, patience can mean, I am cool with the promise that this will happen so I let it go and move on and wait expectantly until the proper timing and manifestation of the thing hoped for.

Waiting can also mean, "What are you willing to give up in order to receive what you want"? Good question, are you willing to give up your own will to get the thing you hoped for? If so, I encourage you to have patience and wait. While you are waiting, get your "house" in order so that you can be found prepared for the thing you need patience for. Remember, I mentioned that being patient does not mean being inactive. Work on something else while waiting so that you can be prepared for the fullness of the blessings you are patiently waiting. This will keep you occupied so that you are not feeling so impatient. Be prepared to have the thing you are praying for in your life. Work on getting your attitude ready, your health better, your finances in order, prepare yourself mentally, and spiritually.

This week's mantra: I am waiting on God, and I move with expectancy.

PROMISE

"And now, O Lord, I am your servant; do as you have promised concerning me and my family. May it be a promise that will last forever." 1 Chronicles 17:23 (New Living Translation)

You will be blessed in the city and blessed in the country. The fruit of your womb will be blessed, and the crops of your land and the young of your livestock - the calves of your herds and the lambs of your flocks. Your basket and your kneading trough will be blessed. You will be blessed when you come in and blessed when you go out" (Deuteronomy 28:3-6).

"The LORD will open the heavens, the storehouse of his bounty, to send rain on your land in season and to bless all the work of your hands" (Deuteronomy 28:12).

These are just a few of the hundreds of promises made by God to us that can be found in the Bible. As you probably guessed, these three are a few of my favorites.

A promise is the assurance that you will do exactly what you said you would do. A promise, like trust, is a two-way street. It takes at least two people to make a promise binding. The person making the promise and the person or persons receiving the promise, all agree to the promise and the stipulations that are included in the promise agreement. If any of the parties involved do not hold up to their end of the agreement, the promise is broken and will not be fulfilled. Like trust, if the promise is broken it can be very unlikely that it is regained easily, if at all.

My father and mother used to tell my siblings and me that once a person loses trust in you, the relationship is damaged, and it will be very difficult to regain their trust back. This is great advice, and I use it all the time. However, God's rule is different. He forgives us, and then He gives us a second chance. Yes, that is good news. But remember, when we mess up, even after we repent, most of the time there are still consequences to pay for our mess-ups.

My parents also taught us to keep our promises, and be trustworthy in every relationship and situation. Do this, and most likely things will work out fine. This is a very short, easy lesson to share and learn. There are no shades of gray. Promises are revealed when promises are kept. There is no other way to see a promise manifested other than to keep your end of the promise in trust and honesty. Otherwise, you forfeit the manifestation of the promise.

This week's mantra: The promises I make to myself and others are better than gold.

INTEGRITY

I know, my God, that you examine our hearts and rejoice when you find integrity there. You know I have done all this with good motives, and I have watched your people offer their gifts willingly and joyously. 1 Chronicles 29:17 (New Living Translation)

Watch over your heart with all diligence, for from it flows the springs of life. Put away from you a deceitful mouth, and put devious speech far from you. Let your eyes look directly ahead, and let your gaze be fixed straight in front of you. Watch the path of your feet, and all your ways will be established. Do not turn to the right nor to the left; turn your foot from evil. Proverbs 4:23-27 (New American Standard Bible)

Integrity, as often heard, many times means doing what is right because it is the right thing to do even when no one is looking. Integrity is so much deeper than just that one definition. I shared two scriptures that talk about integrity. There are many others you may want to read. In addition, here are some rules that help define integrity:

Integrity:

1.Integrity does not just apply to big decisions. It also applies to small decisions. It pertains to your whole life.

2.Integrity is doing the right thing, not necessarily the popular thing.

3.Integrity is being honest, upstanding and having a strong character.

4.Aligning our thoughts, motivations, attitudes, and actions with the ethical principles found in God's Word.

5.Integrity is being honest.

6.Integrity is being truthful.

7.Integrity is doing what God would do.

8.Integrity is doing what you know to be right when everyone else around you including friends, family and loved ones may not agree with you.

9.Integrity is standing in the midst of adversity and knowing that you must abide by God's will, design, and purpose for your life.

10.Integrity is consistency of actions, values, methods, measures, principles, expectations, and outcome. In both our personal lives and our ministry, what we believe, what we say and what we do should be consistent, congruent, reliable, and transparent." (*Wikipedia*)

This week's mantra: My integrity speaks for me!

CHARITY

When you give to someone in need, don't do as the hypocrites do—blowing trumpets in the synagogues and streets to call attention to their acts of charity! I tell you the truth, they have received all the reward they will ever get. Matthew 6:2 (New Living Translation)

Charity is one of the greatest gifts we can give. When I was a child my parents and other people would say, it is better to give than to receive, I thought it was the craziest thing I ever heard. My thoughts were the total opposite; to me it was much better to receive than to give. I was thinking about all of the cool gifts I would get on my birthday, for good grades, Easter and especially for Christmas. Receiving looked pretty good from where I was sitting.

One day, while listening to a sermon for the thousandth time on "It is better to give than to receive," I finally got it. Especially when the pastor posed the question, would you rather give to someone in the hospital or be the person in the hospital receiving. He even took it a little further when he asked would you rather be the person who lost their job and could not afford to buy food, or be the person who gave to the person who lost their job. I chose to be the person who *gave* in each scenario. It wasn't that I decided not to be selfish and help; I decided that I did not want to be sick or without a job so I better give more. Obviously, I still did not get it. Several years later, my true heart took over, and I fully realized why I really believed it was better to give than to receive after the same pastor reminded us how Jesus unselfishly gave His life for us. When I give now, it is only because I want to please God and be a blessing to others that are in need. It is a gift that I am blessed to be able to give to others. When you give based on just wanting to be a blessing to someone and want nothing in return, including public recognition, this is charity.

To me the worse thing anyone can do as it relates to giving is to give and tell everybody that you gave, or even worse, parade the receiver around in front of people and tell the public what you gave to them. This is not charity or being a blessing. This is being prideful. We all know what happens to pride: it goes just before a fall.

I encourage you to find ways to be a blessing to someone each day. It could be a smile, a phone call, a monetary gift, or a word of kindness spoken to someone who is expecting you to be unkind. It could be something as simple as cleaning out your closet and donating items to a homeless shelter, Goodwill or the Salvation Army. How about the next time you are shopping for groceries, pay it forward by secretly paying for someone's groceries in the same line you are in. Try it; you will be surprised by how amazing you will feel after the deed is done.

This week's mantra: My charity begins at home and moves outward to others near and far.

WORK

And since it is through God's kindness, then it is not by their good works. For in that case, God's grace would not be what it really is—free and undeserved. Romans 11:6 (New Living Translation)

So you see, faith by itself isn't enough. Unless it produces good deeds, it is dead and useless. James 2:17 (New Living Translation)

The word *work* means a lot of things to a lot of people. Work can mean the thing you do every day on a job for a paycheck. It can also mean what you do for the kingdom of God. Regardless of the context, the word *work* is used almost always as an action word.

In the Bible, at the very beginning, we can see the importance of work. The second chapter of Genesis teaches us that work is definitely part of God's plan. He did not place Adam in the Garden of Eden to be lazy and idle, or to sit around all day twiddling his thumbs. God expected Adam to work in the garden, to take care of the garden and to make sure all things went well in the garden. *Genesis 2:15 (New International Version) says, "The Lord God took the man and put him in the Garden of Eden to work it and to take care of it."*

Paul says in 2 Thessalonians 3:10-12 (New International Version), For even when we were with you, we gave you this rule: "The one who is unwilling to work shall not eat."

We hear that some among you are idle and disruptive. They are not busy; they are busybodies. Such people we command and urge in the Lord Jesus Christ to settle down and earn the food they eat."

As Christians, we are called to work hard. Whatever work we do, we must work as if we are working directly for the Lord himself.

Then there is work we do according to our faith. The Word of Gods says, "Even so faith, if it hath not works, is dead, being alone" James 2:17 (King James Version. That means you can have all the faith in the world (And you must have faith to get things to happen), you can pray about a thing 24 hours a day without ceasing, wish upon a million stars, and hope for a thing to happen until you are blue in the face. If you do not do the work part, the thing that you have the power to do, you will gain nothing. Your faith needs your works for the manifestation of a thing.

Yet, it is not by our works, so that no man can brag or boast that we are blessed. To some of us, this may sound a little contradictory. I assure you it is not. This particular statement means that you cannot earn your way into heaven nor do enough good stuff to get God's love. It means that only through and by God's grace are we blessed.

God knew that if we could win brownie points with Him we would brag and boost about what we did. We would fail to remember that every good and perfect gift comes from the Almighty. Having said all of this, it still does not give you permission to live a life doing everything and anything you think you are bad enough and bold enough to do. Remember, there are consequences for continually making bad decisions and asking for forgiveness. We should do what is right because it pleases God. And we should want to do good works to please Him because of His unfailing love for us. Just like our children, or like we did as children, we want to do those things that please our parents. We want to make them happy so we do the things they tell us to do, not only because it is the right thing to do, but because we ultimately want our parents' approval. My daily goal is to please my heavenly Father in all I do and say! So I work to build the kingdom and to earn a living each and every day of my life.

I will be the first to admit working hard is not easy, but the results are definitely worth it for me!

This week's mantra: The work I do today is a reflection of my faith.

HOME

Then the father realized that that was the very time Jesus had told him, "Your son will live." And he and his entire household believed in Jesus. John 4:53 (New Living Translation)

And if it seems evil unto you to serve the LORD, choose you this day whom ye will serve; whether the gods which your fathers served that were on the other side of the flood, or the gods of the Amorites, in whose land ye dwell: but as for me and my house, we will serve the LORD. Joshua 24:15 (New Living Translation)

Home is really is where the heart is. And the people who share your home with you are your household. Regardless of your relationship with them, they are a part of your household if they are living there with you. The people who live with you should have some level of responsibility to keep the home tidy and the bills paid if they are old enough to help. This takes some stress off you and teaches accountability.

A great lesson I have learned as an adult is to love and appreciate your home, regardless of where it is located. It does not matter what the address, zip code or which city, we must have pride in, take care of, and be grateful for our home.

Whether you live in a five-bedroom house, or live with a family member or friend, please be grateful. I am not advocating that you live where you do not want to be, forever. I am simply asking you to be thankful for your home. Thankfulness and being grateful for what you have gets you closer to the kind of home you really would like to have. Don't be fooled, whatever problem you may be having with your family or with yourself has little to do with where the home is located than it has to do with you and your decisions and past choices. (This advice is not intended for someone who is living in an abusive situation. If you are living in an abusive environment, please seek professional advice for plans to seek safety for yourself and your children.)

Wherever you live, make it the best home for yourself and your family. I had to learn this lesson myself. A few years ago due to some financial circumstances in my life, I had to move my family into a much smaller house than the one we previously lived in. The house was also much older than our other house and needed some repairs. I thought I was making the best out of the situation. I thought I was grateful. Turns out, I was not practicing what I had been preaching. I was not happy with our "little house" nor was I grateful. I put on a good show for my sons, but deep down inside I was miserable. Looking back, I see why things happened the way they did. I said I was happy and grateful but that was not the truth.

How do I know I was not truly grateful? I can give you an example. When things broke around the house, I took my time or made excuses as to why I did not have them repaired in a timely manner. I now realize, and with much shame, that I did not treat my smaller house like I knew I would treat my larger home. Simply because the house was smaller, I treated it differently. There is no way I would have treated a much larger house the way I treated this house. There are a lot of things I could have done to make our smaller home much better. Yet, as I stated, to my regret, I did not at first. However, here is the good part, after a couple of years passed; I started making most of the needed repairs. I even planted beautiful flowers in the front yard and added some much needed paint to the interior and exterior of our home. Now, I am so proud of my home. It looks so pretty now that the grass is healthy and neatly cut and edged every seven to ten days. Solar lights now outline our walkway! I even make sure the stovetop, cabinets and refrigerator doors are spotless, because let me tell you, some days I had even let the kitchen get out of hand. Every other room was always in shape because you never know when someone might drop by for a visit. I even had the audacity to hold other people's homes and kitchens to a higher standard, because I would never have eaten anything from a stovetop that looked like mine. Yet, I ate food from my kitchen daily.

Thank God for opening my eyes because now I can honestly say, I am thankful and grateful for my house, for my home. I have made the necessary repairs, and I love coming home to my beautiful new home. It is the same, small house, but it is home to me and my boys. I have learned to be more appreciative. I am sincerely grateful for the house I have and we care for it with pride and joy just as we will treat our mansions in the future.

I've often asked people in my workshops that if you do not take care of your small house, or your older model car, what makes you think you will do better in a larger house or brand new car. The bottom line is, the more you value something, the better care you will provide regardless of the number of rooms or the year a car was made. Always remember, home really is where the heart lives. And where the heart is, being thankful and grateful are usually close by.

This week's mantra: My home is a place of comfort and serenity. I am very thankful for my home.

FORGIVENESS

Even if that person wrongs you seven times a day and each time turns again and asks forgiveness, you must forgive." Luke 17:4 (New Living Translation)

Then if my people who are called by my name will humble themselves and pray and seek my face and turn from their wicked ways, I will hear from heaven and will forgive their sins and restore their land. 2 Chronicles 7:14 (New Living Translation)

The most difficult part about forgiveness for probably many of us is to forgive ourselves. Oftentimes, we forgive others for some really painful and sometimes horrific things, but for some reason, it is very difficult to forgive ourselves. It is equally difficult to believe that God forgives us and loves us through it all.

There are many reasons why forgiveness seems so aloof. Sometimes we use unforgiveness as a way to hurt the person who hurt us. Let me tell you, this only hurts the one who will not forgive. While we are up all night wondering why we cannot sleep, sometimes it is because of unforgiveness within our hearts. Believe me, I know from experience what unforgiveness can do in your life. I carried a burden or grudge against someone for many years. The hurt was so deep I just did not want to forgive them, because I thought if I forgave them that meant I had forgotten the pain, and clearly I had not. So I carried the pain and the burden of not forgiving them. However, the person was able to go on with their life and actually became quite successful. I, on the other hand, was the one who could barely sleep at night. Then I remembered something I read about the damage unforgiveness could do to a person. I also remembered an exercise that was suggested on a TV talk show about how to get over the hurt and betrayal by a person you once loved. The therapist suggested writing a letter to that person and telling them exactly how what they did hurt you and how it affected your life. The most important piece to the suggestion was to burn the letter after you wrote it. So I decided that I would try this. I did, and when I read the letter I hit the wall. Not physically, but emotionally. I cried and cried, and then cried some more. After I cried, I received a revelation. I did not cry because of what I wrote, I cried because of all the power I had given to this person. It wasn't so much about the hurt and betrayal, I cried because I had allowed the past to make me bitter, and I let the bitterness change me. I then apologized to myself and asked *me* to forgive *me*. I forgave myself, and then almost simultaneously I finally accepted the person's apology and forgave them. I felt so much better mentally and emotionally. Although I did not start to sleep better at night immediately, after a month or so I did begin to sleep through the night. Forgiveness is powerful, and it cleanses the mind.

Now I am asking you to forgive the people in your life who may have hurt you. I encourage you to please forgive yourself too. Try the suggestion from the therapist about writing the letter; just be sure to burn it afterwards.

This week's mantra: When I forgive others, it opens the door for others to forgive me too.

GRIEF

I tell you the truth, you will weep and mourn over what is going to happen to me, but the world will rejoice. You will grieve, but your grief will suddenly turn to wonderful joy. John 16:20 (New Living Translation)

Grief can be caused by many varied occurrences and situations. The grief I am referring to here is the grief caused by the death of a loved one. We will all experience the death of a loved one at some point in our lives. However, each of us is entitled to, and will, grieve differently. Regardless of what someone tells you, your timetable is your timetable. How you handle your grief is unique to only you. You are entitled to grieve in your own way. Please know that you should be able to ask for any help you may need whenever and as often as you are in need. I encourage you to do what works for you. You will definitely have to identify a "new normal" for your life. Rarely if ever will things go back to "normal" for you.

From my on personal experience, grieving is extremely tough, but God is sovereign. I promise you can trust Him and lean on Him. He understands. You do not have to pull yourself together or say what you think He wants to hear, He cares and He understands your pain. All you have to do, when you can, and when you are ready, is to ask Him to intercede on your behalf, especially when you cannot pray for yourself. God promises to give you beauty for ashes. Trust me on this one; He will do just what He promises.

Since my son, Brandon's, death, I have met many mothers and fathers who have experienced the painful death of losing a child. Before Bran's death, I do not remember having personally met a parent who lost a child. Now I have talked to and shared my story with countless parents, and I pray that somehow I was able to comfort them, if only for a moment. I also hope that I was able to remind them of God's love for them and to reassure them that God is strong enough to carry them through. He understands our pain and will gladly bear our burdens.

I know that grief can sometimes overwhelm us, especially on holidays, birthdays, special occasions and at family gatherings, so I encourage the parents to please honor how you are feeling and pray for strength and guidance, so that the grief does not cripple you emotionally or spiritually. I further share that time and fervent prayers will help heal the wounds of grief. And I ask and pray that you will allow family and friends to be there for you, when they offer, as long as it is what you want at the time. You make the decision when you are ready, and have someone you trust completely to assist you in the areas you need help in the most. Grief seems to have more power over us especially when we are alone. Please allow a trusted friend or relative to sit with you or just hold the phone with you are on the other end instead of always being alone during this time.

This week's mantra: God's grace is sufficient for me. He always carries me when I am too weak to stand.

HAPPINESS

Those who love money will never have enough. How meaningless to think that wealth brings true happiness! Ecclesiastes 5:10 (New Living Translation)

So I recommend having fun, because there is nothing better for people in this world than to eat, drink, and enjoy life. That way they will experience some happiness along with all the hard work God gives them under the sun. Ecclesiastes 8:15 (New Living Translation)

Let's start with my statement of truth as it relates to happiness: Happiness is a choice, and should not be based on feelings or how much money you have.

One of the toughest questions I have ever been asked is, "What makes you happy?" I venture to say this question is also tough for many other people too. If your happiness is based on things outside of your spirit of influence, then you are bound to experience less happiness than the person whose happiness does not constantly depend on external indulges. What is the real secret to being happy, regardless of outside indulgences? Glad you asked; the secret is to embrace joy.

Joy is the power to be all right, regardless of outside influences. I shared earlier in Week 3 why having joy is better than being simply happy.

Having said all of that, I mentioned earlier that I have been asked often what makes me happy and that this question is a tough question to answer for me. It is deeper than just deciding to choose joy over happiness. Well I usually tried to change the subject, or simply answered, pleasing God, my sons and my job. Then the questioner would often say, "Loretta, other than pleasing God, your sons and your work, what makes you happy? What do you enjoy doing in your spare time? "What do you do for fun?" I would continue to prove to them that my sons and my job truly make me happy. I am happy spending time talking to my sons and going places with them. I am happy when I can pay all of my bills on time. I am happy when I talk to and see my mom. I am happy when I talk to my brother, my sister, and my friends. I am happy when I am not talking to anyone. I am happy being alone. I am happy in a crowd. I am happy in the morning. I am happy at night. Basically, I am a happy person.

This worked for me until a professional therapist asked me the same question and wanted an answer other than my "stock" answer of pleasing God, my sons and my job. She stated that those things that make me happy involve other people. She wanted to know what I did just for me. I answered, I really do not know. I told her I have never taken the time to find out. She was saddened by this information. And when the impact of my answer hit me, I was saddened to, because I know God wanted more for me. And this sad new revelation brought tears to my eyes and the therapist eyes too. That conversation inspired and challenged me to find out what brings me happiness outside of what I do for others.

So, I decided to go on a soul-searching tour to discover what really makes me happy. During this time, I re-addressed the differences between happiness and joy and quickly decided to rephrase the question and my quest to discover what I like to do just for fun, since I already knew where my joy comes from and what brings me happiness.

What makes me happy? Doing the things that help me become more of the woman God create me to be. Learning things to help me become a better daughter, parent sister and most of all a better mom to my sons! What brings me joy? Knowing that I have the grace, mercy, favor, and love of God each and every day really comforts me. I am joy-filled when I wake up in the morning, and immediately I thank God for waking me and allowing me to see another day. I am joy-filled when I realize how blessed I am to be able to be a blessing to others through my friendships, speaking engagements, books and my TV talk show. I am filled with joy every moment that I remember to be thankful and grateful for all I have and for the blessings yet to come.

What do I do just for fun? I have regular appointments at my favorite hair salon, gym and spa; I go to concerts, museums, parks, movies and plays. I play tennis, I sing, I dance and I travel just for fun. And this makes me very happy knowing that finally, I do things just for me too, and not just for work, my family or friends. Remember, because I now have a healthy self-love and apprecia-tion for Loretta, I am obligated to take better care of me.

This week's mantra: I am enjoying my life by being happy, having fun and joyful!

DISORDER

For God is not a God of disorder but of peace, as in all the meetings of God's holy people. 1 Corinthians 14:33 (New Living Translation)

For wherever there is jealousy and selfish ambition, there you will find disorder and evil of every kind. James 3:16 (New Living Translation)

Which comes first? Does internal disorder, i.e., depression, lack of peace, weariness, mental fatigue or external clutter, i.e., in your home, car, office, unorganized, chaos, and messy spaces appear first? This is another million-dollar question. My answer is two-fold.

I believe that we are not only physically connected to our houses, cars, desks and office, but we are also spiritually connected to those spaces.

Therefore, when the spaces that we occupy daily are cluttered and unorganized, it introduces clutter into our psyche. Furthermore, I believe that when we are troubled, worrying or depressed it introduces clutter into our physical spaces. When I am challenged emotionally or spiritually, I have noticed that I have a tendency to not keep my physical spaces organized or clutter free. My desk becomes messy, the laundry piles up, I may allow the dishes sit in the sink unwashed and my car may suffer as well.

When our minds are cluttered and our physical spaces are filled with clutter too, what should we do?

In order to break that cycle, regardless of what became cluttered first, our psyche or our physical space, we have to create and implement a plan to de-clutter and get organized.

Being organized is crucial to spiritual, physical and mental success at work, home and in our community. Here are simple steps to help on the road to becoming more organized. (Note: It is a great benefit if we encourage everyone in the household to get involve too.)
•If you turn the light on, turn it off when leaving a room.

•It you open a door, as soon as you are finished with the task that caused you to open the door, close the door.

•Make a place for everything, and put everything in its place.

•If you bring in new items, you should throw an old item out.

•Pay your bills on time. Create a system and implement it monthly.

•Return phone calls and emails at a scheduled time.

- •Keep your appointments. Rescheduling takes up more time and can cause tension.

- •Throw out trash as soon as you are finished eating. Do not let trash and paper build up in your car. Throw it out.

- •Read mail daily. Immediately throw away pieces you do not need.

- •Make a folder for all of your important papers and store the papers in a file.

- •And lastly, purchase organizing items, i.e. plastic bins, boxes and file folders.

Many professionals agree that it takes at least 21 days for a new routine to become a habit, so please don't become discouraged if everyday things are not done according to your plan. Just right the wrong as soon as you notice the deviation from the plan to become and stay organized!

You will appreciate the hard work and commitment to organization each time you come home and everything is neat and in order. You will definitely notice that your car appears to ride better when it is clean inside and out. I know I do!

This week's mantra: I have peace in my heart and mind, therefore my external space is peaceful too!

DEPRESSION

"And now my life seeps away. Depression haunts my days. Job 30:16(New Living Translation)

Come quickly, Lord, and answer me, for my depression deepens. Don't turn away from me, or I will die. Psalm 143:7(New Living Translation)

For the sake of this message about depression, I am referring to a temporary feeling of hopelessness, inadequacy and constant worrying. Let me emphasize, I am not referencing the clinical definition of depression. Nor is this information intended as a professional diagnosis or advice. However, regardless of the cause of depression or the severity, God can heal and restore your mind and heart. God hears your prayers and will answer you. Additionally, please know that He does equip professionals to assist in the healing and restoration of your mind, body and heart.

Depression is a thief and a liar. It can ruin your day and your life, if you let it. The best way to defeat depression is to deal with the cause of it early on. Face your fears. Speak life into your life. Believe what God says about who you are. Replace the negative messages with the word of God. Tune out the negative channels that call you out of your name. You can change your thoughts and the messages. You must choose to stop negative behaviors and messages daily. What message would you send to your best friend or relative if they were feeling and thinking depressed thoughts? Chances are you would speak lovingly and kind words to them. You would remind them that you love them and want the best for them. These messages are the exact messages you should say to yourself as well.

From time to time, most people experience events that may cause them to be depressed. Being aware of and admitting that you may need professional help is one key to becoming mentally healthy. This awareness is strength, not a weakness. If you were not feeling well physically, most of us would go see a doctor, and we would not consider this as a weakness. The same wisdom should apply if we are not feeling our best mentally; we need to see a doctor. Do not self diagnose. If something does not feel right mentally or physically, see a professional.

This week's mantra: God's spirit within me rules. And I am protected from the spirit of depression. I am mentally and physically healthy!

PLANS

For I know the thoughts and plans that I have for you, says the Lord, thoughts and plans for welfare and peace and not for evil, to give you hope in your final outcome. Jeremiah 29:11 (Amplified Bible)

There are the plans we make, and then there is the plan of God. Just like most of us make travel plans, vacation plans, girls' night out plans, guys' night out plans, family reunions, and plans to improve our lives. I pray that all of us would be bold enough to seek out opportunities to help build a successful retirement plan. Create a plan to develop a nonprofit organization or a foundation that will help assist others in their times of need.

I would go even further and ask that we, those who are interested, become entrepreneurs whether full-time, part-time, or on an as needed basis.

I further suggest that at the very least, we encourage our children, our youth to create and own their own businesses too. One of the best ways is to encourage them to choose an industry they would like to work in, learn all they can about that industry, and then seek volunteer to work there and then chart a course to one day become an employee there or own a similar business.

The interesting point I want to make is having a plan is only a small part of living your dreams. Once you have your plan, the second step is writing the plan down. And the third and most important step is to execute your plan. In order to experience success you must work your plan. An extremely significant part of your plan is assigning each step a time frame for completion. This helps ensure that you are on schedule for accomplishing your plans.

When executing your plan, another nugget of truth I discovered is to be very flexible. Plans should not be carved in stone. As the word states, only God knows the plans that He has for each of us.

So continue to be mindful that God has a greater plan for your life, so that you can be in alignment with His plan while you are creating your own specific plan.

This week's mantra: My plan is good, but God's plan is greater! I choose God's plan.

LEGACY

Don't you see that children are God's best gift? The fruit of the womb his generous legacy? Like a warrior's fistful of arrows are the children of a vigorous youth. Oh, how blessed are you parents, with your quivers full of children! Your enemies don't stand a chance against you; you'll sweep them right off your doorstep. Psalm 127:3 (The Message)

Legacy is what we leave behind to our children and the world. It can be as broad as wealth and as certain as good health and reputation. Good or bad, negative or positive our life will leave something behind for the next generations to come. Choose wisely, what your legacy will be.

I had the opportunity to interview on my TV show, Michael V. Roberts, owner of the Roberts Companies. To give you a glimpse of how successful he is, a lot of people compare his wealth and knowledge to that of Donald Trump. Mr. Roberts and his brother, own close to one hundred different businesses, including three television stations, 11 hotels and the Roberts Orpheum in St. Louis, Missouri. Mr. Roberts was asked by another interviewer why he names all of his businesses "Roberts". He responded by saying that it is funny how he gets asked that question; yet no one ever asks the Rockefellers, the Hiltons, or the Fords why they named their businesses by their last names. I was deeply inspired by his profound response. Another profound statement Mr. Roberts shared with us was on legacy, and I will never forget it. He also added, "What some call ego, will be legacy in a few years."

So whether or not you can leave behind a legacy of wealth and prestige to your family, you are definitely going to leave a legacy; I pray that it is one you will be proud of.

My goal is to leave a legacy of integrity, massive wealth and a successful and an easily duplicated model of philanthropy so my children and my children's great grandchildren will be blessed.

This week's mantra: I will leave a legacy of wealth, integrity, spiritual wisdom and philanthropy that will be available not only for my grandchildren but also for my grandchildren's grandchildren.

CELEBRATE

"His father said, 'Son, you don't understand. You're with me all the time, and everything that is mine is yours—but this is a wonderful time, and we had to celebrate. This brother of yours was dead, and he's alive! He was lost, and he's found. Luke 15:31 (The Message)

For most of us, I do not think we celebrate our life, children, or accomplishments enough.

Celebrations do not have to break the bank or be extravagant in nature. Celebrations should be held more often. I believe a good way to show how grateful you are for reaching a goal is to celebrate each accomplishment along the way.

Celebrations can be done in many ways. They can consist of just doing something special for yourself like dinner at your favorite restaurant. Or it can be as elaborate as throwing your 50th birthday party on a cruise ship or you can invite family and friends over to help you celebrate the anniversary of the day you decided to become healthier and fit.

A celebration can also be something totally relaxing, like snuggling up on the sofa with your favorite book or listening to your favorite song.

I invite you to decide to schedule more celebrations in your life.

Celebrations can be a form of praise. So get your praise on, celebrate the fact that you are reading this book. Celebrate that you are on your way to living a more joy-filled life! Celebrate having *faith for the next step!*

This week's mantra: I have so much to celebrate! I am so grateful for all I have today!

TRUST

The Lord is my strength and shield. I trust him with all my heart. He helps me, and my heart is filled with joy. I burst out in songs of thanksgiving. Psalm 28:7 (New Living Translation)

Commit your way to the Lord; trust also in him and he will do this: He will bring forth your righteousness as the light, and your justice as the noonday. Psalm 37:5-6 (New American Standard Bible)

But as for me, I am like a green olive tree in the house of God; I trust in the lovingkindness of God forever and ever. Psalm 52:8 (New American Standard Bible)

These verses describe the place I want to be in my trust in the Lord. I want to truly and completely trust Him with all my heart, all of the time.

Trust is a big issue for me. It is one of the most difficult things for me to try when it comes to delegating responsibilities or meeting new people. I even learned that I had trust issues with God. Oh my. Dare I admit this personal truth? As I looked back over my life, several areas in my life shouted that my trust in God was sporadic at best. In some areas I trusted Him completely, and other areas I did not.

Trust means that I have faith in Him, that I am totally and completely dependent on only Him 24 hours a day every day. I expect Him to be available for me all of the time. It means that I count on Him for everything, that He loves me unconditionally, and that His word is true. At different times of my life, I noticed sometimes my faith was stronger than at other times, I was totally dependent, I believed He loved me unconditionally and yet other times there were many moments of doubts and disbelief that God would answer my prayers or that He truly cared for me. It was like a rollercoaster ride. What I know now for sure is random trust is not the kind of trust my Heavenly Father deserves. He deserves all of my trust, faith, dependence, expectation, love and belief that He is who He says He is. That's the "trust Him with all of my heart" trust Psalm 28:7 (New Living Translation) is referencing. And that is the kind of trust that I am aiming for moment by moment. I am definitely closer to that level of trust than I have ever been. I choose to trust God in all things with all of my heart all of the time.

This week's mantra: I completely trust in God's will for me, knowing His will is for my greater good.

PRAYER

And all things, whatsoever ye shall ask in prayer, believing, ye shall receive. Matthew 21:22 (King James Version)

There are three things I know for sure about prayer. First, prayer is simply a two-way conversation with God. Secondly, sometimes the thing we need to do the most during our times of despair, sadness, mourning, happiness, change, trials, and tribulations is to pray. But very often prayer is the thing we want to do the least. And thirdly, one of the principles of answered prayers is when you pray, you <u>must</u> believe that you will receive what you pray for.

There are many lessons I have learned about prayer, and they are what I subscribe to wholeheartedly.

1. We are to always pray without ceasing.

2. Prayer without works is useless.

3. "The prayers of the righteous availeth much". Notice it does not say the prayers of the perfect, it says the righteous. Thank God for that!

4. Prayers are heard and answered. Yet, not always in the manner or timeframe in which we hoped but they are answered nonetheless.

5. When praying, it is wise to spend time listening too.

Here is a formula or acronym I learned from my pastor, Craig Strickland, when I first started attending Hope Presbyterian Church:

A.C.T.

Acknowledge the goodness of the Lord. Speak to him about how good He is all the time. Include some of the things He has done for you.

Confess any sin or weak areas in your life and pray for forgiveness, wisdom and guidance.

Thank God for your blessings and for being so good. Choose a time when He worked something out for you or when He did something that you never expected in your life. Tell Him about it and then, say Thank You.

And the final step is to simply state your request, and talk it over with God and before closing, say, in Jesus name, Amen! I make it a practice to **A.C.T.** sometimes without asking for anything but forgiveness. Some days instead of praying a prayer of request, I just say nothing more than these three words, Lord, thank you!

To help me make this transition of a new prayer life, I liken it to what if my sons talked to me only when they wanted to ask me to do something or give them something. I recall how it would make me feel. So how much more do I owe to my heavenly Father, than to just adore Him, praise Him and worship Him more than I ask Him for things whether for others or for me. I owe Him so much more than that. He is a good God. Prayer is my conversation with Him anytime, and as often as I make the time, He listens and He cares. In Jesus' name. Amen!

This week's mantra: Dear God, may you be pleased with the words from my mouth and the song of my heart every day.

Seasons

And God said, Let there be lights in the firmament of the heaven to divide the day from the night; and let them be for signs, and for seasons, and for days, and years: Genesis 1:14 (King James Version)

For everything, there is a season, and a time for every purpose under heaven: *Ecclesiastes 3:2 (American Standard Version)*

There really is a season for everything under the *Son*. (Not a typo. Well originally, it was but when I got ready to change it, I felt intuitively that it was really not a typo after all.) One of the principles to living a more joy-filled life is, sometimes you have to know what season you are in and what to do in that particular season. There are typically four seasons of life just like the four seasons of nature.

Spring-Planting, sowing seeds. *Giving time.*

Summer–the heat is turned up, but it is needed to grow into the person we were created to be. *Growing time.*

Fall–Harvest time. The seeds we sowed and planted are ripe and time to harvest. *Receiving time.*

Winter –Being patient, standing, waiting on the Lord. *Waiting time.*

Being able to identify which season you are currently experiencing is not always easy. Because one thing I know without a doubt, God can bless you and will bless you in any of the seasons. God is not limited by anything. So a season of winter can have some spring like qualities. Even in the summer, you can harvest a blessing. So be very careful in determining which season you are in. Another thing to watch out for is duration. Only God knows the timeframe for our seasons in life. For example, I have seen it snow in early November and late spring. I have experienced lack one day and the very next day abundance. Again, God is not limited by space or time.

With that information, I encourage you to look for His goodness and guidance each and every day. No one can determine what season you are in, only our heavenly Father can do that. I have only been able to accurately determine my seasons many years later, after the fact. I do know, without any reservations, each season is necessary for the growth and development of our body, mind, and soul according to God's plan for our lives both now and eternally. Embrace each season, and you will blossom just like the beautiful flowers, plants and trees!

This week's mantra: I am thankful for the season I am currently experiencing. For I am growing into the person I was created to become.

Disappointment

And this hope will not lead to disappointment. For we know how dearly God loves us, because he has given us the Holy Spirit to fill our hearts with his love. Romans 5:5 (New Living Translation)

I have yet to meet one person who has not experienced disappointment at least a few times in their life. I do know that disappointment can prove to be very powerful but only if you allow it to be. It is a fact that disappointment is a *reaction emotion* caused when we are hurt, whether intentionally or unintentionally by people we love, or by strangers. Sometimes certain outcomes from our decisions that are not in our best interests may cause disappointment. The defense to this reaction emotion is to choose a different response. Try not to become emotionally tied to the outcomes.

When you are disappointed, the first response is usually very negative. You may want to physically or emotionally hurt the person that you feel let you down. You may even want to completely give up on what you were hoping to accomplish. These negative responses are never the right thing to do, although you may feel like going this route at that time.

We have the power to choose which emotions we display in response to whatever has happened in our life, whether we deemed it negative or positive. Just as we can choose to respond in a negative manner, we can choose to respond in a more positive manner as well. Not to speak lightly on disappointments, I know it hurts, been there done that, and will probably experience disappointment after disappoint again. However, I will consciously choose to display a healthier response and emotionally disconnect to the unfavorable results.

One thing is for sure, sometimes in our life we will experience many disappointments, during these times I encourage you to take a minute or two before you respond to whomever or whatever caused the disappointment. Take this time to pray for wisdom. If you begin to practice this strategy, I promise you will be on your way to a more joy-filled life.

Sometimes things just don't work out according to our plans. In times of disappointment, I recite Jeremiah 29:11 (the New Living Translation) *"For I know the plans I have for you," says the Lord. "They are plans for good and not for disaster, to give you a future and a hope."* When things do not turn out exactly like I planned, I simply ask for God to give me wisdom, and I develop a different plan, because for me, giving up or quitting is never an option.

This week's mantra: I will not feel disappointment or discouraged, for this too shall pass. I am the apple of my Father's eye!

76

SERVICE

God has given each of you a gift from his great variety of spiritual gifts. Use them well to serve one another. 1 Peter 4:10 (New Living Translation)

"You are the light of the world. A town built on a hill cannot be hidden. Neither do people light a lamp and put it under a bowl. Instead they put it on its stand, and it gives light to everyone in the house. In the same way, let your light shine before others, that they may see your good deeds and glorify your Father in heaven. Matthew 5:14-16 (New International Version)

In order to lead, one must first have a heart to serve others. Great leaders are great at serving others. Of course service can mean a lot of things to a lot of people. For me, service means first humbling myself to be able to do any task that I may ask someone else to perform. Also, service means if I am needed to be in the background or behind the scene as a worker, I can do that too. If I need to volunteer to clean the bathrooms at church then I can do that also. If I am needed to be a guest speaker in front of thousands, I can very humbly do this. If I am asked to set up chairs for a meeting, I will happily setup the chairs.

Most times a good leader operates as the leader, and leads others to meet a common goal. He or she gives the orders, creates the plans and receives all of the acclaim when plans are successful. A good leader may or may not share the blame when things do not go as planned. A good leader does not serve others, they simply do the job of leading.

However, a great leader knows that he must serve first before he can successfully lead his team. A great leader can be seen working side by side with his team whenever needed. A great leader has empathy and compassion for the team. A great leader takes responsibility when something goes wrong. A great leader shares the acclamation and success with their team.

The Bible tells us that Jesus led thousands by example, yet, He became the greatest servant this world has ever known. And His steps are those I choose to follow. I am His humble and blessed servant!

This week's mantra: I am a great leader, because I am a humbled servant first. I serve others with humility, respect, dignity and integrity.

Worry

Worry weighs a person down; an encouraging word cheers a person up. Proverbs 12:25 (The Message)

"So don't worry about tomorrow, for tomorrow will bring its own worries. Today's trouble is enough for today. Matthew 6:34 (The Message)

When you go through deep waters, I will be with you. When you go through rivers of difficulty, you will not drown. When you walk through the fire of oppression, you will not be burned up; the flames will not consume you. Isaiah 43:2 (New Living Translation)

Remember the song, "Don't Worry Be Happy"? The entire song consisted primarily of those four words, *Don't Worry Be Happy*. Millions of minds were changed, and countless unnecessary items were sold with the same slogan from this song, which is rarely played at all on the radio anymore.

Although we remember the song, the words are so critical to having faith for the next step. Worry and being faithful are not synonymous. If you are faithful, quite clearly you are not worrying. And if you are worrying, you quite clearly are not faithful.

From a spiritual perspective, there is a quote that says, "If you pray, don't worry and if you worry, don't pray."

Worrying is connected with sleepless nights, negative habits, bad decisions, medical and mental illness. These things, when combined with other stresses and disappointments, may lead to hospitalizations or worse.

I worried so much until I started worrying about worrying so much. Then I worried even more because I was worrying way too much. However, there is an obvious solution to worrying.

What I learned over the years, after thousands of hours of worrying, is that, for me, worrying was a sign of a lack of faith. Oh my, not me, I have loads of faith, right? Well, the proof is in the pudding-sleepless nights, mild hypertension, weight gain and crankiness.

It took fervent prayers and daily reading of the Bible to help me realize the only cure for worry was faith. Which simply meant; I had to believe without any doubt, that God will always be there for me, and that He knows what is best for me. And this knowledge and belief, was the cure of my worrying. Upon doing further research I found that about 90% of the stuff we worry about never ever happens.

This week's mantra: Don't Worry Be Happy!

EDUCATION

*The wise accumulate knowledge—a true treasure;
know-it-alls talk too much—a sheer waste. Proverbs
10:14 (The Message)*

A quality education is definitely an equalizer. And the
good news is education is available to all who pursue it.
It can be the difference between having a lucrative ca-
reer and having a job. Education can sometimes be the
difference in being highly successful and prosperous or
just merely getting by financially.

Another much used quote is "knowledge is power". I
heard people add, yes, knowledge is power, but the
use of that knowledge is more powerful. I've added,
"and the sharing of knowledge is world changing!"

I want you to know that I have heard and disagree with
the statement college is not for everyone. Let me tell
you this, some form of higher education is definitely for
everyone. Be it business school, trade school, typing
school, cooking school, modeling school, online school,
how to bake a cake school, how to repair a car or truck
school, there should be more education for everyone
past high school. The more education and knowledge

you have the better your chances of getting a particular high salary job or starting your own business.

The most successful people will always admit that they are life-long learners.

Intellectual property is the most valuable property on the earth. Not even the most expensive properties in California or New York combined can compare in value.

To quote my father again, "No one can take your education away from you. The banks can't take it away, it cannot be repossessed nor can it be stolen from you once you get it. Your education will last forever".

Always challenge yourself to learn something new and positive every day. Use the knowledge to educate and empower someone else along the way.

This week's mantra: I am a life-long learner. And I share my knowledge with others.

WISDOM

The Lord was pleased that Solomon had asked for wisdom. 1 King 3:10 (New Living Translation)

God gave Solomon very great wisdom and understanding and knowledge as vast as the sands of the seashore. 1 King 4:29 (New Living Translation)

For wisdom will enter your heart, and knowledge will fill you with joy. Proverbs 2:10 (New Living Translation)

What is the difference between wisdom and knowledge? Knowledge is what you learn or earn by reading and experiences, either your own or that of others. However, true wisdom comes only from the Lord.

To me wisdom is better if you compare the two. When King Solomon was asked to ask for anything he wanted, he asked God for wisdom. And "God said since you did not ask for the death of someone or for the worlds' riches," he granted his request. He also granted Solomon with much wealth.

Since I believe God honors those who ask for wisdom, I choose to ask daily for God's wisdom in every situation I face.

We cannot go wrong as long as we follow God's directions. I want to share with you, there have been many times that I made my own choices without first seeking God's wisdom, and of course you guessed it, things did not turn out as well as they would have had I chosen to seek the wisdom of the Lord.

This week's mantra: Today, I choose God's wisdom first, and then I choose knowledge.

PATIENCE

Finishing is better than starting. Patience is better than pride. Ecclesiastes 7:8 (New Living Translation)

Here is where I get to confess to you that patience is not a virtue for me yet. I am claiming patience in the areas where I need it daily.

I would like to begin this message by saying I believe that a lack of patience is interconnected with your current measure of faith. I am so guilty of praying for something to happen when I know that the timing was probably not right. There have been many times I have tried to manipulate a situation or person(s) to get my way. I know that you are shocked. Me-manipulate someone? Well, in a good way. I do not try to ever take advantage of anyone, yet I have taken advantage of some situations to get my way, in my time. I admit that when this happened I cheated myself out of what God would have done for me had I not taken matters into my own hands. Had I been patient, I am sure things would have been much better. I am often guilty of trying to help God be

God, when I know, without a shadow of doubt, that God is God all by himself. As I stated in the beginning, I am unquestionably a work in progress. God is not through with me yet.

Trust me when I tell you that God does not need our help to make things happen for us. Have you ever prayed for something and even left it at the altar, but then you went back and got it off the altar? Well, I have countless times. I remind you, and me, God does not need our help. This does not mean you should be standing idle doing nothing. It simply means that you should not try to force something to happen or try to manipulate the situation or people to make things happen faster than God wants it to happen.

Have patience, God is never too late, not even one second late.

Another lesson I have learned about patience is be very careful of what you pray for when it comes to patience. *Note to self*, patience can only develop under pressure!

So, if you really want patience, then pray for patience, but if what you are really seeking is guidance for making a situation become better or you want release from a stronghold, then pray very specifically for guidance and release.

This week's mantra: I am grateful that God's timing is perfect all the time.

Week 33

Blessings

I will make you into a great nation. I will bless you and make you famous, and you will be a blessing to others. Genesis 12:2 (New Living Translation)

The blessing of the Lord makes a person rich, and he adds no sorrow with it. Proverbs 10:22 (New Living Translation)

What does it really mean when someone says, "I am blessed?" I suppose that I should define the word blessing. A blessing can be the approval of a thing; it can be something tangible or intangible. One thing is for sure; blessings are gifts from God.

Blessings come in many shapes, forms and sizes. I am sure I have missed out on some blessings, because it did not look like I thought it would look. Maybe I rejected it because it did not sound like I wanted it to sound. Do not be tempted to discount something or someone that could be a blessing in your life simply because it does not look or sound like you thought it should.

The Bible says that every good and perfect gift comes from God. I also had to realize that God uses people to bless us. I cannot count the number of times I turned down blessings because of pride, or I just told the person that offered to help me that "everything is okay you do not have to do that or give me that". Huge mistake. My selfishness and pride may have stopped someone from receiving a blessing when I would not allow them to bless me.

Take it from me, the next time someone offers to give you something that you have been praying for and/or need, please allow them to bless you. It all comes from God.

Disclaimer, I am not talking about when a teller or cashier gives you too much money back. I don't believe God works like that. That teller or cashier will be in trouble if their cash drawer is short and could potentially lose their job. Or the person in front of you accidentally drops money on the floor and you pick it up and put it in your pocket. This does not sound Godly to me. I pray that if this ever happens to you, you will do the right thing and give that money back.

This week's mantra: My blessings do not hinder another person's wellbeing. My blessings will enrich me and others.

ASPIRATION

The aspirations of good people end in celebration; the ambitions of bad people crash. Proverbs 10:28 (The Message)

Wishing and simply wanting something to happen or change will not garner the results you are seeking. Aspirations are goals that you create to get to an expected outcome. They can be short-term or long-term goals. I encourage you to start setting and achieving your personal and professional goals today.

Until you write down on paper the things you aspire to accomplish, they are just wishes. Not until you take the time needed to write them down and apply action steps and a timeline will they become your goals in life. There are many areas that we can set goals in, however, here are examples of goals in my five favorite goal areas and an example of each goal:

1. Spiritual–I want to learn more about God's plan for my life. I will read the Bible more and I will do this weekly until I have memorized all scriptures related to God's plan for my life.

2. Physical–I want to be at my ideal weight for my height by my next birthday. I will exercise 3- 5 days a week for 45 minutes. I will count my calories to make sure I do not exceed the recommended amount to lose the unwanted pounds and to maintain my ideal weight. I will eat foods that are more nutritious every day.

3. Financial–My goal is financial security. I want to have a savings account that maintains a six-figure balance, and I want to have several sound investments that also produce seven figure profits annually. I will pay my tithes each week and give to the three charities of my choice annually.

4. Mental–Starting now, I will spend time mediating daily. I will schedule my "me time" appointments and keep them every two weeks.

5. Professional–I want to become a multibillionaire media mogul, and provide hundreds of well paying jobs. I will grow the show to national syndication and become a New York Times best-selling author. I will accomplish this goal in the next 5 years. I will also build a successful charity.

And once you accomplish your goals, remember to have a celebration for each one. And then consistently create new goals in other areas of your life.

This week's mantra: I will achieve all of my goals according to God's plans for me.

EXERCISE

You've been raised on the Message of the faith and have followed sound teaching. Now pass on this counsel to the followers of Jesus there, and you'll be a good servant of Jesus. Stay clear of silly stories that get dressed up as religion. Exercise daily in God—no spiritual flabbiness, please! Workouts in the gymnasium are useful, but a disciplined life in God is far more so, making you fit both today and forever. You can count on this. Take it to heart. This is why we've thrown ourselves into this venture so totally. We're banking on the living God, Savior of all men and women, especially believers.
1 Timothy 4:6 (The Message)

Whether spiritual or physical exercise, I liken exercise to a secret crush; it can be the most kind and elusive of any relationship. And if we don't do the right things to develop the crush on something or someone, it will always be just a crush and not fully a real relationship. But a relationship, nonetheless, that we each must develop and then nurture at least three to five times a week for 45 minutes to an hour, depending on our fitness goals. Like me, you have probably started more exercise routines than you can count. Routine of course, is the operative word.

What I have discovered is that the exercise concept and health benefits have to be embraced first. The only way that I have been able to sustain any form of relationship whether family or friend, is to first embrace it. The word relationship is a noun but to be successful at it, it has to be treated like a verb, an action word just as exercise is action, requiring movement. It also has to be learned, courted, and ultimately committed to for life. It will accept nothing less in order to produce the results we need. Exercise indeed has to be treated like any other successful relationship that endures the test of time.

We must devote and set aside time to exercise just like we would for someone we deeply love and care for. Based on my personal experience, on the days that you really do not want to or simply do not feel like exercising, it is during those times that you benefit from exercising the most.

Another lesson I have learned is exercise will not give you the results you want, if you are not consistent. Believe me; I have tried it many times for years. Inasmuch as I would like to tell you that once you reach your desired weight, or you have accomplished your goal of walking/running your first marathon, you are finished; I cannot encourage you to stop. You should not stop exercising. If you stick with your plan of exercising at least three to five days a week for at least 30-45 minutes a day, after a while, and it varies from person to person, your body will actually start to crave exercising. I know it sounds a little crazy, but rest assured, it can happen for you too, if you continue to consistently exercise until it becomes a habit for you.

And like any new relationship, you will learn what works and what does not work for you. Also remember to keep your routine refreshed so that you will not become bored. As I stated earlier, exercising is a relationship. So go out and find a exercise routine that is both fun and challenging that you can fall in love with for a lifetime. You may not enjoy exercising each and every time, but the results will be the same if you stick to your plan, to become a healthier you.

This week's mantra: Each day I am becoming more spiritually and physically fit!

HEALTH

The picture of good health, vigorous and fit. Job 21:24 (New Living Translation)

Do you know your health status? The only way to truly know for sure if you are indeed a picture of health is to know your numbers. I am not referring to your phone number, Social Security number or even your favorite numbers; I am asking you to find out your BMI (body mass index), heart rate, blood pressure, waistline and current weight. These are some of the most important numbers to know when gauging how healthy you are. Depending on these numbers, your doctors can tell you if you are at risk for heart disease, hypertension, certain cancers and diabetes. These ailments are the leading causes of death in the United States.

Your age can also be a factor in being diagnosed with the above illnesses. Even if you are, diagnosed with any of the illnesses listed, help, better health and life-saving changes are a doctor's visit and treatment away. Eating a healthy balance of fruits, vegetables, proteins, carbo- hydrates and taking vitamins daily, combined with a consistent exercise routine, can also be beneficial to having good health.

Minimizing the stressors in your life can also help to improve your numbers and your health. I am aware that a lot of people say, "well I will just pray about it" and of course I am a huge advocate of prayer, and I also believe God gives health professionals wisdom to aid in the treatment and cure of all manner of sickness. Ultimately, it is your personal decision how you handle your healthcare. So, as you are praying please pray for wisdom and knowledge as to what God will have you to do!

Disclaimer: This information is based on my own personal experiences, research and approach to becoming healthier. I am not a healthcare professional, so please seek professional advice from your doctor to get on the right track to better health.

This week's mantra: I exercise and eat healthy everyday to ensure that I am very healthy!

FASTING

"And when you fast, don't make it obvious, as the hypocrites do, for they try to look miserable and disheveled so people will admire them for their fasting. I tell you the truth that is the only reward they will ever get. Matthew 6:16 (New Living Translation)

If there ever was a forgotten art, for me it would be fasting. I have read a few books on fasting. I have heard of the countless benefits of fasting, yet it is a practice that I have not championed as much as I probably should. There are several types of fasts. Only you can determine which one works best for you after you have completed your research. I have come to believe that fasting has spiritual, physical and mental benefits. It can teach us discipline, obedience, focus and the value of sacrifice. Let's visit each one separately.

Discipline–sticking to a plan for the agreed upon time frame and not being easily swayed to quit no matter the circumstance or reward.

Obedience–doing things without seeing the mutual benefit immediately or at all; being committed to something without expecting a benefit to you.

Sacrifice–giving something to someone else knowing you really wanted it for yourself; doing something for someone so that they are happy, knowing that it takes away something from you or your plans; the giving away of one's possessions, time or talent without any expectations in return

Focus-not being easily side tracked or enticed to give up until the job is totally completed in excellence. Your plans or thoughts and actions are not all over the spectrum; not leaving one thing unfinished before moving on to something else prematurely before the first task is completed.

Another critical piece of information I learned about fasting is that it includes more than merely fasting from food. Fasting can be very inclusive. I have been on food fasts and I have also given up watching TV, being on the computer, talking on the phone, asking for things every time I pray, and a negative thinking and speaking fast.

The lengths of fasts are as numerous as the types of fasts. I have fasted for hours, days and weeks. However, the common denominator result from fasting for me has always been clarity, restoration, peacefulness, and calmness. I know the Bible states that when we fast, we do not have to announce it to the world, or do some physical action to show that we are fasting. I believe fasting is definitely a personal form of worship. I further believe fasting is a very intimate agreement between the Father and His child. I also embrace and appreciate the value of corporate fasts.

This week's mantra: I give up any and all things and people who hinder me from being my best.

SUCCESS

Common sense and success belong to me. Insight and strength are mine. Proverbs 8:14 (New Living Translation)

Potiphar noticed this and realized that the Lord was with Joseph, giving him success in everything he did. Genesis 39:3 (New Living Translation)

Like beauty, I believe success is in the eye of the beholder. Success means many different things to many different people. I think that success should be defined by the beholder and not by the person looking in from the outside. Wisdom tells me that allowing someone else to define what success is for me is giving them too much of my personal power. And I believe, defining success solely in terms of the accumulation of material things, i.e. owning expensive cars, houses, designer clothes and shoes is not true success.

Of course, to some, success is the opposite of failure. I have heard and now agree with Mr. Michael Roberts, CEO of "The Roberts Companies", philosophy about failure. He said, "There are no failures, only experiences."

This statement has truly empowered me and changed my way of thinking. It has helped reshape the way I look at my life both personally and professionally. I am convinced that if we take another look at what we once deemed failure, I am sure you will agree with me, and Mr. Roberts, that "there are no failures, only experiences. So in essence, as long as we continue to pursue success, the worse thing that can happen is we gain more experiences. This newfound knowledge helps prove my father's philosophy: experience is one of life's greatest teachers.

I have also heard that failure is just success turned inside out, another brilliant nugget of truth for me. So let me encourage you today, persistently pursue your dreams and eventually you will experience lots of success!

This week's mantra: I have the power within me to create success I am successful in all I do!

Week 39

WORSHIP

"Everything on earth will worship you; they will sing your praises, shouting your name in glorious songs." *Interlude Psalms 66:4 (New Living Translation)*

Worship the Lord with gladness. Come before him, singing with joy. Psalms 100:2 (New Living Translation)

I have three questions to ask regarding worship: How, where and when do you worship? The question of when is the easiest of the three for me to answer. When: As often as possible. Where: Wherever you feel comfortable.

Now, let's discuss the "how". Well in my opinion there are at least three different forms of worship. This takes a little more time to explain. Worship can be done verbally in private or in public, silently, in certain gestures or in song. Which forms you choose is completely your decision, I encourage you to worship daily.

Worship is simply expressing your love, adoration, thankfulness and gratification to God. This can happen through song, dance, words, silence, singing in the choir, the way we work, the way we interact with others, the way we share with others, the way we spend our money, save our money, give our money and share our money can all be a form of worship if we do them in excellence to please God.

Sometimes, worship is private and sometimes it is very public! I have embraced the fact that my worship may not look or feel like anyone else's definition. I have accepted this fact. I have felt total peace and joy singing worship songs at home lying on my sofa, and I have felt the same level of peace during my early morning daily prayers. At church, while the praise team and choir are singing, just the notion of joining my voice with theirs gives me the same comfort and peace as we all worship together.

I believe the way I parent my sons is a form of worship. I believe being patient and spending time with my mom is a form of worship, especially the times when I am spending time with her just because she is my mom. I also believe reading my Bible and mediating on God's Word is worship. Just to learn more about Him is worship. I equally believe doing all of these things out of mere obligation is the opposite of worship.

Spending lots of quality time alone with God and studying His word for growth and answers can help you create your many forms of personal worship.

Lord, we honor and worship you for the ability to know more about you! Lord, we worship you simply because you are our Father.

Loretta McNary

This week's mantra: Living my life to be a blessing to others is a form of worshiping my heavenly Father!

PRAISE

Praise the Lord! Give thanks to the Lord, for he is good! His faithful love endures forever. Psalm 106:1 (New Living Translation)

Let them praise the Lord for his great love and for the wonderful things he has done for them. Psalm 107: 8 (New Living Translation

In my personal quest to understand the art of praise, I learned that for me, ultimately my praise should be continual. I then created my personal definition of praise, a seamless and simultaneous transition from praying to extolling God for being God. My praise does not come with a button that can be turned on or turned off. I believe being committed to continual praise will lead to a ceaseless and perfected praise. Likened to breathing, you do it without even thinking about it. Praise is being thankful in action, silence or verbally. It is the flawless motion of going from prayer to praise, which for me is the ultimate form of true worship.

You may wonder if there have ever been times in my life when I could not or did not want to praise God.

Well, the answer is yes. There have been instances when I was too weary or too depressed to praise our awesome Father. Yet, even in my darkest situation, eventually I realized that my heart and soul would praise Him, even when my mind could not or would not. I have noticed on several occasions when I was too weak spiritually or mentally to praise Him, He filled my spirit with His Holy Spirit and sent me a praise through the remembrance of a melody of a song. And as I began to hear the song in my heart, I would then begin to sing the song. And before I recognized what was happening, I would begin to offer praise to the Lord in song for that song. This opened my heart to praise Him even more until I was no longer feeling weak or depressed about the situation. Once I began to remember all of the things I had to be thankful for; and stopped focusing on the negative, my outlook changed. So in essence, many times "my praise found me."

Offering praise to our Father is being thankful regardless of what the circumstances are and how things look with the natural eye. It is knowing within your heart that your prayers will be, and already are, answered.

You might ask, how do you offer praise? Well, here is how, you offer praise through prayer, through meditations, singing songs of praise and/or through dance. Yes dance! The Bible says King David danced as a sign of praise.

Another way to give God praise is through the things you do. Give God the glory and honor by doing your very best in everything you do. This is a great way to praise Him.

This week's mantra: May the joy I feel everyday be revealed in my praise.

GIVING

Give and you will receive. Your gift will return to you in full—pressed down, shaken together to make room for more, running over, and poured into your lap. The amount you give will determine the amount you get back. Luke 6:38 (New Living Translation)

As a youth, I did not understand completely what it meant by the statement, "It is better to give than to receive." As a young girl, I thought that receiving was the better of the two. Gifts are what I thought everyone wanted all of the time. Now that I am an adult, I understand that it is much better to give than to receive. I would much rather be on the giving end most of the time. However, I realize that you must also allow others to give to you as well.

I was of the mindset that being independent meant that you did not accept any help from others because it was a sign of weakness. Now, I recognize that this was unhealthy thinking. Asking and allowing someone to help you in a time of need is strength. Anything less can be interpreted as pride.

Giving in time of need or just to show appreciation to someone is an absolute admirable quality to possess. Remember, gifts come in various forms; it does not necessarily have to be strictly monetary.

Regardless, of how much money you have or do not have, there is always a way to help someone. For one, have a genuine desire to truly want to help, and you will find a way or the way will find you. Secondly, be willing to give with no plans or desires to be repaid now or in the future.

This week's mantra: Planned giving is great, but unexpected giving is greater.

Finances

For the love of money is the root of all evil; and while some have coveted after it, they have erred from the faith and pierced themselves through with many sorrows. 1 Timothy 6:10 (21st Century King James Version)

Our self-worth and value should not be defined by our finances or perceived lack of enough finances. Remember you are a worth more than gold. In order to not fall in the category of being a lover of money, we should all agree that money is only a means to an end. And having lots of money should not be our primary pursuit in life. Instead, we should work toward having healthy financial outcomes. Finances are more than just the money you currently have or wish to have. Your financial portrait should also include how you currently save, spend, and lend your money. Finances also should consist of how you use your time, your talents, and any investments you may have i.e. stocks, bonds, intellectual and physical property.

It can be somewhat difficult to increase our finances especially if we do not find ways to educate ourselves on the successful strategies of managing all of our assets and how to identify and reduce our liabilities. The future of our finances also depends on educating ourselves on how to get and keep wealth. Our present financial picture was painted by our past decisions; and if we are to become more victorious in the future we should focus on making better informed decisions when it relates to generating and maintain wealth.

How can we change our financial outlook for the future? I recommend this easy step: Create a monthly budget. Budgeting is like a sword. It can cut coming and going especially in the beginning when we are starting from scratch.

We have to take a serious look at how much money we make versus how our money is currently being spent. This transparency may cause anxiety because we may discover that our expenses exceed our income.

However, budgets are very crucial to the success of our financial security. Budget planning should be very personal and should not be a one size fits all formula. While one budget plan may produce tangible results fast for one person, another person may use the exact same budget and may not reap any results.

Having said all of that, creating a budget and sticking to it is key to saving money, and having a healthy and secure financial future.

Here are a few tips on creating a budget that have worked for me and hopefully with a little tweaking, they will work for you too:

- Identify all of your expenses and income. Knowing exactly where and how your money is being spent will help you stick to your budget.

- Create a spreadsheet and or a folder to use for your budget.

- Set a goal for your savings and one for becoming debt-free.

- Talk to a professional credit counselor if you need to.

- Address self-address envelopes for each accounts for each month.

- Choose which day of the month to mail your invoices and include the check or money order along with the invoice. Be sure to include your account numbers on each money order or check.

- Keep all receipts in a separate envelope or a box for tax purposes. I make a copy of my receipts, because the ink may start to fade after a few weeks. Attach the receipt to the copy of the receipt you make.

- Lastly, teach everyone in your household to create and manage their own budget using your tested procedures.

A word of encouragement, let a trusted person know where all of your pertinent personal information like check books, insurance papers, titles, deeds, passwords, spare keys are kept in case of an emergency.

As I stated at the beginning, finances are more than just money.

This week's mantra: My self-worth is not defined by my bank account. I only make informed decisions regarding my finances.

COMPLIMENTS

Kind words are like honey—sweet to the soul and healthy for the body. Proverbs 16:24 (New Living Translation)

When she speaks, her words are wise, and she gives instructions with kindness. Proverbs 31:26 (New Living Translation)

Mark Twain once said, "I can live two months on a good compliment." This quote helps prove my point of how important it is for us to say something nice to ourselves and to others daily. Here is a tip: When giving a compliment please always make sure the compliment is true and has merit. Do not get in the habit of passing out trite compliments unless you want to receive trite compliments in return.

One interesting fact that I have found to be true about compliments is men are much better receivers than women are based on my personal observations. When a man receives a compliment, he is quick to agree and say thank you. On the other hand, when a woman receives a compliment she is quick to talk down the compliment. So my advice to the women who do this: When someone gives you a compliment, please just say "thank you". You do not have to tell them that the dress is really old or that the shoes were actually purchased from the goodwill, or I got this on sale; just simply say thank you.

In our everyday interactions with people I am sure that if we search deep enough you can find something good about each person for which you can pay them a compliment, even if they are not some of your favorite people, One of my favorite adages helps to prove this concept, "Give credit where and when credit is due."

Maybe you like the color blouse or shirt someone is wearing or the smell of their perfume or cologne. Perhaps you have not seen them in a while and you are glad to see them again. You should tell them. Or maybe you like the way they handle themselves in a crisis, or you really enjoyed the speech they gave please make an extra effort to tell them.

Compliments are like encouragement; we all need to hear compliments sometimes. Furthermore, if no one pays you a compliment, compliment yourself. Also an equally important rule; never withhold a compliment as a form of punishment.

Make a point to compliment several people each day. This not only makes others feel great, you will start to feel great too. Again, only give compliments that are genuine.

This week's mantra: I will speak words of kindness to others and to myself.

Week 44

STRENGTH

In your strength I can crush an army; with my God I can scale any wall. 2 Samuel 22:30 (New Living Translation)

And he said unto me, My grace is sufficient for thee: for my strength is made perfect in weakness. Most gladly therefore will I rather glory in my infirmities, that the power of Christ may rest upon me. II Corinthians 2:19

Strength like patience is a commodity that we find we have more of when we need it the most. Strength is not usually measured unless we are in times of trials and tribulations. I have second-guessed my level of strength many times. I even questioned whether I would have enough strength and faith to finish this book. I wondered if I have enough strength to do all of the things on my to-do-list today. I doubted that I would have enough strength to overcome different challenges in my life. Perhaps you have asked the same questions. I can say with total confidence, that yes we do and yes we will have the strength we need every time we need it. God's word promises that we will. See the scriptures above as a reminder.

Strength is never-ending and unrelenting when called upon. But like hope and joy, you have to seek it out and you will find that it will not disappoint.

If you are presently going through a tough or stressful time right now, I believe for you, and with you, that you are strong enough to handle it as long as you do not give up. Seek the Lord, pray about the situation, and believe that God's strength is perfected when you are weak. My dad used to tell me more times than I can remember, "What doesn't kill you only makes you stronger." I have often asked out loud, "How strong do I need to be?" I am still unsure of the correct answer, but I am sure about God providing the strength we need to endure any and all circumstances. I am further convinced He will continue to supply the strength we need. There is no limit or lack in God. So don't ever hesitate to ask for His strength as often as you need to.

This week's mantra: Whenever, I need it, God's strength is always available for me.

Loretta McNary

Week 45

PARENTING

Now I am coming to you for the third time, and I will not be a burden to you. I don't want what you have—I want you. After all, children don't provide for their parents. Rather, parents provide for their children. II Corinthians 12:14 (New Living Translation)

I believe being a parent is the most difficult job anyone can have. I also believe that there is nothing more noble, rewarding and enjoyable than being a parent for those who choose to, and/or are blessed to be a parent, whether biological or otherwise.

Children are always a blessing to us. They are so precious and deserve loving, caring parents who shield and protect them and provide a safe and nurturing environment each and every day. We are their role models. It is our responsibility to provide for them, set boundaries and instill morals and values in their lives. We are their first teachers. Let's be sure to teach them the value of education and the value of respecting and loving others.

As parents, we have to understand that successful parenting mostly comes by trial and error. At this date,

117

there is no scientific formula or plan to ensure our success as parents. We have to admit that sometimes we do not always get it right. Sometimes we might make the wrong decision; sometimes we may even make a mistake. I believe that one of the worst lessons we can teach a child is that parents don't make mistakes nor do we admit we made a mistake to them and in front of them. This oversight can set them up for repeating our mistakes. Let's teach them accountability by admitting to them we made a mistake and apologize when a mistake is made.

My heart and prayers go out to all those who desire to and are trying to become parents but have not been able to conceive. I have read and heard about countless stories of parents who once believed and were told that they could not have children and now they have several; either by adoption or biologically or a combination of the two. God has the last say so. And furthermore, regardless of what the present circumstance are today, always follow your heart. Ask the Lord to lead, guide and direct your steps. I further pray that you have peace and joy within always. And may you always have the courage and *faith for your next step as parents.*

This week's mantra: May I learn to parent like my heavenly Father parents me.

 the

Loretta McNary

Week 46

OBEDIENCE

Everyone has heard about your obedience, so I am full of joy over you; but I want you to be wise about what is good, and innocent about what is evil. Romans 16:19 (New International Version)

Even though Jesus was God's Son, he learned obedience from the things he suffered Hebrews 5:8 (New International Version)

Behold, to obey is better than sacrifice...I Samuel 15:22 (King James Version)

What is obedience? Obedience is being submissive to the will of God every time, especially when it is an inconvenience to you. Obedience pleases God. God's Word tells us that obedience is better than sacrifice. When you are obedient you give up your will for God's will.

Abraham is one of the greatest examples of an obedient servant. God asked him to offer his son Isaac as a sacri-

119

fice. You may have heard or read the story of how Abraham took Isaac up the mountain to make a sacrifice of him. Just as Abraham was about to put the knife in his son's heart, God stopped him and pointed to a ram stuck in a bush nearby. Abraham was rewarded for his obedience, and the ram was offered up as the sacrifice in Isaac's place.

Wow! That is obedience. I pray to become more obedient everyday. I hope you will join me.

Side bar: Another powerful nugget I learned while studying Abrahams life is: when he and Isaac where traveling to Mount Moriah, Isaac asked "where is the lamb"? And many generations later, that question was answered. Jesus, the Lamb of God was sent to this world and was used to pay the ransom for us.

This week's mantra: May my will always bow to the will of God.

Week 47

CHILDREN

Her children rise up and call her blessed; her husband also, and he praiseth her saying: Proverbs 31: 28 (American Standard Version)

I truly believe that all children are a gift from God. I also believe that it is our duty and responsibility to ensure that they are loved, cared for, protected, sheltered, inspired, empowered, and educated on a daily basis. It is our job to provide food, shelter and a safe, loving home and environment.

We are to train them to be good citizens, respectful and kind to others and to obey authority. We are to set boundaries and enforce rules and moral values. If as a child for whatever reason you were not provided these rights and privileges as a child, then you owe it to yourselves, and your children, to seek out parenting organizations, training, resources, and professional agencies that can help. The Bible states it this way, "Train up a child in the way he should go and when he is old he will not depart from it." This means that they will not forget the values and morals we taught them, even though the circumstances may look as if they have, based on some of their decisions. Like we did when we were younger, they feel as if they have all of the answers. And that we as parents and adults do not understand what they are dealing with at the time.

Raising our children is not something we should try to do alone; it really does take a village to raise a child, especially if a child is to grow up healthy, well rounded and happy. Another valuable lesson I learned as a parent is to apologize to our children when we make a mistake or have been a little too harsh with them. I think this tip is invaluable to parenting our children. It lets them know that we are human and we sometimes make mistakes too.

As you can imagine, the advice and opinions relating to parents and parenting is as numerous as the grains of sand in the desert. There are literally thousands of books written on the subject of raising successful and healthy children. There are thousands more on how to be a great parent using various proven techniques and styles. The best suggestion I can make is find out what works best for you and your family. What I have learned is usually a parent uses the methods their parents used that they now appreciate, and scrapped the methods their parents used that did not produce the best results at the time.

One book other than the Bible that really helped mold and shape my parenting style the most is "The 5 Love Languages" by Dr. Gary Chapman. In his book, Dr. Chapman describes what he believes to be the most common personality types and the best ways to parent based on the child's personality type.

Dr. Chapman's books are really a great read and offer sound advice and principles for raising happy, productive and loving children into successful, healthy, well-balanced community leaders.

This week's mantra: My children will call me blessed.

CHANGE

Jesus heard about it and spoke up, "Who needs a doctor: the healthy or the sick? I'm here inviting outsiders, not insiders—an invitation to a changed life, changed inside and out." Luke 5:31 (The Message)

There are three things you can depend on that will happen in all of our lives.

- •Taxes
- •Death
- •Change

Change is inevitable. It happens more often than we like. And it is rarely ever anticipated. One thing that's for sure, we will experience little, to no growth, without change. There are several things you can do when change invades your space,

- •Roll with the flow and grow
- •Fight against it, or

•Deny it exists

Regardless of what you choose, change happens. You can either let it affect you negatively or choose to respond in a positive manner and embrace the changes. I recommend the latter.

Motivational speaker and author, Jim Rohn, says, "Change begins with choice." Rohn states, "Any day we wish; we can discipline ourselves to change it all. Any day we wish; we can open the book that will open our mind to new knowledge. Any day we wish; we can start a new activity. Any day we wish; we can start the process of life change. We can do it immediately, or next week, or next month, or next year. We can also do nothing. We can pretend rather than perform. And if the idea of having to change ourselves makes us uncomfortable, we can remain as we are. We can choose rest over labor, entertainment over education, delusion over truth, and doubt over confidence. The choices are ours to make..."

Let me encourage you to allow the changes happening in your life, especially if you want different results from what you are currently experiencing. Change starts with one decision at a time and one day at a time.

This week's mantra is the Serenity Prayer

God grant me the serenity
to accept the things I cannot change;
courage to change the things I can;
and wisdom to know the difference.
Living one day at a time;
enjoying one moment at a time;
accepting hardships as the pathway to peace;
taking, as He did, this sinful world
as it is, not as I would have it;

trusting that He will make all things right
if I surrender to His Will;
that I may be reasonably happy in this life
and supremely happy with Him
forever in the next. Amen.

GROWTH

Don't be misled: No one makes a fool of God. What a person plants, he will harvest. The person who plants selfishness, ignoring the needs of others—ignoring God!—harvests a crop of weeds. All he'll have to show for his life is weeds! But the one who plants in response to God, letting God's Spirit do the growth work in him, harvests a crop of real life, eternal life. Galatians 6:7 (The Message)

Growth, like change, can happen whether you want it to or not. Sometimes it happens even if you do nothing to acquire it.

Growth sometimes is very painful mentally and spiritually. Just like a diamond has to have the impurities burned from it, we have to experience some things in our lives that are challenging, yet yield a more refined person after the refining process. I can tell that I have gone through some changes that felt like I was in the refiner's fire every time. And in actuality I was. I did not agree with the process while I was going through, but I

can definitely say, I am much better than I was before I
went through the experience. I am stronger, wiser and
so much better, just like the words to one of my favorite
songs, "Never Would Have Made It" by Marvin Sapp.

Just like we do as parents, family and friends, we tend
to think we know what is best for those we love. Sometimes our knowing and the processes we use to prove
our point, hurts the ones we are trying to love and protect. Yet, we know when this phase is complete, they
will be so much better. God is like that. He knows what
is best for us, even though when we are going through
the refining process it feels like pain. Rest assured that
God is right there with us and, we will be so much better after the test.

Change equals amazing growth, and growth equals a
more qualified, faithful equipped servant. After all,
this is what we pray for, right?

*This week's mantra: Today I am new and improved! I em-
brace the positive changes in my life.*

Acceptance

This saying is reliable and worthy of complete acceptance by everybody. 1 Timothy 4:9 (Amplified Bible)

One thing is for sure, the act of acceptance has to be chosen, it does not come uninvited, nor does it dwell where it is not wanted. Here is a story I read by an unknown author that exemplifies what true acceptance really means:

I recently completed my college degree. The last class I had to take was Sociology. The teacher was absolutely inspiring with the qualities that I wish every human being had been graced with. The instructor's last project for us was called "Smile." The class was asked to go out and smile at three people and document their reactions. I am a very friendly person and always smile at everyone and say hello anyway, so I thought this would be a piece of cake. Soon after we were assigned the project, my husband, youngest son, and I went out to eat one crisp March morning. It was our way of sharing special time with our son. We were standing in line, waiting to be served, when all of a sudden everyone around us began to back away, and then even my husband did. I did not move an inch. An overwhelming feeling of panic welled up inside of me as I turned to see why they had moved. As I turned around I smelled a horrible, dirty body smell. There, standing behind me, were two, poor, homeless men.

As I looked down at the shorter gentleman closest to me, he was smiling. His beautiful sky blue eyes were full of God's Light as he searched for acceptance. He said, "Good day" as he counted the few coins he had been clutching. The second man fumbled with his hands as he stood behind his friend. I realized the second man was mentally deficient and the blue eyed gentleman was his salvation. I held my tears as I stood there with them. The young lady at the counter asked him what they wanted. He said, "Coffee is all, Miss" because that was all they could afford. If they wanted to sit in the restaurant and warm up, they had to buy something and they just wanted to be warm. Then I really felt it -the compulsion was so great I almost reached out and embraced the little man with the blue eyes. That is when I noticed all eyes in the restaurant were set on me, judging my every action. I smiled and asked the young lady behind the counter to give me two more breakfast meals on a separate tray. I then walked around the corner to the table that the men had chosen as a resting spot. I put the tray on the table and laid my hand on the blue-eyed gentleman's cold hand. He looked up at me, with tears in his eyes, and said, "Thank you." I leaned over, began to pat his hand and said, "I did not do this for you. God is here working through me to give you hope." I started to cry as I walked away to join my husband and son. When I sat down my husband smiled at me and said, "That is why God gave you to me, honey, to give me hope." We held hands for a moment. At that time we knew that only because of the grace that we had been given, were we able to give. We are not church goers, but we are believers.

I turned in my Smile project, and the instructor read it. Then she looked up at me and said, "Can I share this?" I slowly nodded as she got the attention of the class. She began to read and that is when I knew that we, as human beings and being part of God, share this need to heal people and be healed. In my own way, I had touched the people at the restaurant, my husband, son, instructor, and every soul that shared the classroom on the last night I spent as a college student. I graduated with one of the biggest lessons I would ever learn—unconditional acceptance.

What a wonderful and remarkable story this woman told. She experienced firsthand what acceptance means.

Because we were given free will, we are not forced to accept certain things in life or certain people for that matter. However, every person was created by God and has inherent value; which means that they deserve to be treated with respect and accepted for who they are in Christ.

Acceptance does not always mean approval. We can accept people that are different from us, yet not approve of how they live or some of the decisions they make in life. It is never our job to judge one another. The Bible says, if you judge, you will be judged by the same manner.

This week's mantra: I pray for my eyes to see others as God sees us. He always sees the best in us.

SACRIFICE

I beseech you therefore, brethren, by the mercies of God, that ye present your bodies a living sacrifice, holy, acceptable unto God, which is your reasonable service. Romans 12:1 (21st Century King James Version)

Sacrifice is one of the supreme decisions we could ever make, but it is also one of the most complicated decisions to make most of the time. Yet, the decision to sacrifice something gives us far more than the thing we gave sacrificially. In my personal experiences, it has always been the finest decisions I ever made.

If a person with a great paying job and lots of money only gave a dollar in church today, they would not be heralded as a hero, actually they would probably be considered a farce. Why? Simply because the person only gave a little, even though they probably had more to give, yet they did not because of selfishness and not out of reverence to God and His promises. Giving the small amount to the church did not hurt their finances or household at all. Therefore, their giving was not recognized as a sacrifice. In my opinion, a sacrifice is something you give even though it is something you would rather have for yourself or the giving will put you further behind financially, but you give so that someone else will be blessed.

The reason why the story of the widow in the Bible is such an inspiration and an awesome example of true sacrifice is because she gave all of the money she had in the world. Her giving definitely had a negative impact on her finances and her household. However, she gave anyway knowing it was her very last. And her actions made her a hero and a prime example of what true sacrifice looks like for all of us to follow.

To know if you are making a sacrificial gift or just merely making a donation, ask yourself if this gift is from the heart or simply from your wallet.

This week's mantra: I pray that if someone needs my last dollar, I will give it freely, without a second thought.

FELLOWSHIP

Those who obey God's commandments remain in fellowship with him, and he with them. And we know he lives in us because the Spirit he gave us lives in us.
1 John 3:24 (New Living Translation)

Fellowship is communing with God and/or with like-minded believers, but can also include unbelievers. When we are intimately aware of and acknowledge God's presence, we are in fellowship with Him. Amazing fellowship can take place in church and outside of church. The key is, when we fellowship, keep Jesus in the fellowship. It is about Him, not about our wish lists or our personal needs. Fellowship includes but is not limited to prayer, reading scripture, praise, and worship, giving to others or sharing our testimonies in church. Of course, most of the time when we think of being in fellowship, we usually think of being in church only. And being in church worshiping with others is a grand example of fellowship. However, that is not the totality of fellowship. Fellowship can be just sitting with a friend listening or simply just being there quietly with them. Fellowship can also include getting together with our family and friends sharing our food and talking about current events or sports. Fellowship can be as simple as hanging out with friends enjoying a movie or play and being thankful that we have each other.

As long as we recognize that God is omnipotent and the Holy Spirit lives within us, and we keep the lines of communication open with Him, we are always in fellowship, even when we feel alone. This realization can make a big difference when we desire to keep our bad moments from turning into bad days.

When we are obedient and keep a consistent, healthy, and committed relationship with Him, we will always be in fellowship with Him.

Every healthy relationship we encounter during our moments and days on this earth are just the icing on a good homemade caramel cake of fellowship.

When you are down, alone, discouraged, disappointed, and want to hide under the covers and never come out, remember you are in continual fellowship with your heavenly Father because His Spirit lives within you and me always.

Another awe-inspiring benefit of being obedient and in fellowship with our heavenly Father is it produces faith for our next step!

This week's mantra: I am basking in the knowledge that I am in fellowship with God. And His Spirit lives in me.

Notes

Notes

Notes

Notes

Notes

Notes

Notes

Notes

Author's Words

I wanted to write this book to share the many lessons I have learned over the years that have been the most therapeutic for me, in hopes that they will be spiritually and mentally therapeutic for everyone who reads this book. I learned that a lot of things that I experienced had placed a negative stronghold on my mind. Now I am totally convinced that through all of my ups and downs I was developing *Faith for the Next Step*. Using the information gained from my valuable lessons taught me not only how to take one day at a time, but how to live in peace and joy every day.

Sure, I have been blessed to accomplish a lot of wonderful things in my life, and with God's grace I have overcome a lot of negative things, but I assure you it has not been without pain, self-doubt, sacrifice, disappointments, discouragement and a lot of obedience. The only reason I am able to succeed is due to God's amazing mercy, love, guidance and forgiveness.

Additionally, the writing of this book was necessary because of my heart's desire to share with you how I learned to survive my bad moments by faith so that my bad moments no longer had the power to turn into bad days.

As with everything that I am blessed to do and say, I pray that every person who reads this book will be more blessed for having decided to share his or her time and energy reading *Faith for the Next Step, 52 Messages to Inspire and Encourage*.

I also pray that if and when my story is ever told, I want it publicly known and stated, that I always practiced thinking positive, dreamed BIG, and I helped someone along the way! And I had faith for my next step!

God's blessings, continual favor and increase in your life overflowing!

"$\mathscr{L}$"

About the Author

Loretta McNary is a successful TV Talk Show Host, a highly requested empowerment speaker, business consultant, advocate and philanthropist. She has been in the communication and broadcasting industry for over 20 years. She has hosted several popular TV and radio talk shows and is currently the host and Executive Producer of The Loretta McNary Show and she also is a host for *On Cable Tonite*, a TV talk show broadcast on Comcast. Her mission is to inspire, educate, motivate and encourage everyone, especially youth, to live a joyful, well-balanced and productive life.

Loretta wants everyone to know her TV shows are a gift from God. Everyone who knows her will tell you that out of all of the amazing things she gets to do, her favorite job is being a loving mother to her five wonderful sons. She is also the founder of PINK EAGLES, a non-profit, leadership development, social etiquette and training organization for girls. PINK EAGLES has been adopted by the Shelby County Sheriff's Office. Loretta is the former Project Coordinator for IMPACT, a Girls, Inc. Memphis project (Infant Mortality Public Awareness Campaign of Tennessee), a teen led initiative. Loretta has received many awards and accolades for her work and community service. To name just a few of her most recent awards, she was selected as one of 50 Women of Excellence 2011 and nominated as a 2011 Children's Champion and MIFA's "Something Good in Memphis" Award 2011.

Loretta enjoys spending quality time with her sons. She is very active in her community and her church. She has been president of the PTSA at her sons' schools several times. Loretta is an avid volunteer for various non-profits. One of her favorite affirmations is "Success comes to me because I live and operate in a No Excuse Zone, and I lead by helping others first." Loretta leads by example and believes in order to be a great leader; one must first learn to serve with humility and empathy.

In February 2011, another one of Loretta's big dreams came true. Loretta received media credentials to cover the Oscars® Setup at the Kodak Theatre in Hollywood, CA. and to be on the Red Carpet inside the beautiful Beverly Hills Hotel in Beverly Hills, California to interview academy award winning actors and actresses at the Night of 100 Stars Oscar's Viewing Party. The show has also received credentials for the "Show Me Music & Art Fest 2011, featuring the hottest performers in country music, and credentials for the Black Enterprise Magazine Entrepreneurs Conference in Atlanta, Georgia.

Additionally, within its first year, The Loretta McNary Show received credentials to cover the Stellar Awards in Nashville (2008, 2009, 2010, 2011), the Image Awards in Los Angeles (2008, 2010), the Kentucky Derby (2009) and the Academy of Country Music Awards in Las Vegas (2009). Loretta has interviewed well over 250 superstars in music, TV, education, healthcare, fashion designers, sports and Film. A few of her absolute favorite interviews so far include the one-on-one interviews with the talented actor, Denzel Washington in Los Angeles and her interviews with Loretta Devine, Ed Asner and Gloria Allred.

Contact the Author
loretta@lorettamcnary.com
facebook.com/lorettamcnaryshow
twitter.com/lorettamcnary
www.LorettaMcNary.com

Loretta McNary
c/o Loretta McNary Studio
6116 Hickory Ridge Mall
Suite 268
Memphis, TN 38115

Book Order Form

Quantity	Description	Cost	Total
	Faith For The Next Step	$14.95 ea.	

BOOK SHIPPING INFORMATION
PRINT PLEASE

Name_____

Address_____

City_____

State/ Zip_____

Email _____

Phone (+ area code)_____

Money orders or cashier's checks only	Total
Subtotal	
S&H (add to total)	2.25
Taxes (If applicable)	
Total amount enclosed	

Make money orders and cashiers' checks
payable to Loretta McNary
mail to
Loretta McNary
c/o Loretta McNary Studio
6116 Hickory Ridge Mall
Suite 268
Memphis, TN 38115

Thank You for Your Support

www.ingramcontent.com/pod-product-compliance
Lightning Source LLC
LaVergne TN
LVHW021453080426
835509LV00018B/2266